by **Deanna Keahey** and **Steve Kilner**

www.maccheese.com

First published in the United States of America
by Plexcentric Publishing in 2004.
Copyright © 2004 Plexcentric Corporation.

Plexcentric Publishing
130 Cora Court
Walnut Creek, CA 94597
www.plexcentric.com
e-mail: inquiries@plexcentric.com

Text by Deanna Keahey and Steve Kilner
All photographs by Steve Kilner and Deanna Keahey

Library of Congress Control Number: 2002116521
ISBN: 0-9725008-0-4

First printing, 2004
Printed in China

Acknowledgements and Credits

Many people have been involved in the production of this book – we'd like to thank all of them for their hard and creative work:

BOOK DESIGN, LAYOUT, & WEBSITE DESIGN	**Christine Daughtry** – www.daughtry.ca
COMIC ILLUSTRATIONS & COMEDIC ASSISTANCE	**Murray Lindsay** – www3.telus.net/mlindsay
BOOK LAYOUT ASSISTANCE	**Laura-Lee Kelley** – www.heavensangelgraphicdesign.com
COOKING AND RECIPE ASSISTANCE	**Chris Dziengeleski**
COVER DESIGN	**Kathi Dunn** - www.dunn-design.com
COVER COPY AND BOOK TITLE	**Graham Van Dixhorn – Susan Kendrick Writing**
EDITING & PROOFREADING	**Rob Chirico, Delores Keahey**
CONSULTING ON PUBLISHING	**Kristen Lewis** – www.upperaccess.com, and
	Pete Masterson – www.aeonix.com
WEBSITE PROGRAMMER	**Bud Salvetti**
COMEDY CONTRIBUTERS	**Mark Levitt** – *Can't We All Just Get Along, The Big Date (Al Dente), TV Interviews, Frankenstein & Igor, Food Pyramid, Psychiatrist, Yankee Doodle* – www.marklevitt.org
	Scott Magri – *Mac & Cheese Cologne, Psychiatrist, Mice and Mousetrap, World Tour*
	Sue Thurman – *Dinosaur Extinction*
	Ed Nickum – *Genie and Wishes*
	Monika McGee – *Mrs. Camembert's Dance School*
	Cameron Kilner – *World Tour*
	Matthew Kilner – *World Tour, Cow Gene Transplant*

(All other comics by Steve Kilner; comic editing and interpretation by Steve Kilner and Murray Lindsay.)

ENJOY

~~WATCH WHAT YOU EAT~~

HAPPY FOOD-HAPPY YOU

Table Of Contents

When You've Got the Time,
Think Outside the Box:
Homemade Mac & Cheese

They're Hungry and You've Got
No Time: Mac & Cheese
Packages and Quick Hits

When It's Mac & Cheese for
Lunch and Dinner

Mac & Cheese Bits and Bites:
Appetizers, Sides and Salads

Beginnings and Endings
with Mac & Cheese

Mac & Cheese Bloopers
and Other Oddities

Easy Recipe Finder

Homemade Mac & Cheese

	Page	Boxed/ Homemade	Time	Vegetarian/ Meat	Kids Specials	Good For Company	Good For Leftovers
White sauce	8	Homemade only	1 hour	Vegetarian	Often liked by kids	Good for entertaining	Works well as leftovers
Layered	8	Homemade only	1 hour	Vegetarian			Works well as leftovers
Custard	9	Both	1 hour	Vegetarian			Works well as leftovers
Stovetop	9	Both	30 minutes	Vegetarian			Works well as leftovers
Microwave	10	Homemade only	30 minutes	Vegetarian			Works well as leftovers
Crockpot	10	Homemade only	More than 1 hour	Vegetarian			Works well as leftovers
Four cheese	11	Homemade only	1 hour	Vegetarian	Often liked by kids	Good for entertaining	Works well as leftovers
Canned soup	11	Homemade only	15 minutes	Vegetarian			Works well as leftovers
Low fat	12	Homemade only	1 hour	Vegetarian			Works well as leftovers
Cottage cheese	12	Both	1 hour	Vegetarian			Works well as leftovers
Soufflé	13	Homemade only	1 hour	Vegetarian		Good for entertaining	
Our favorite mix & match version	21	Homemade only	1 hour	Vegetarian	Often liked by kids	Good for entertaining	Works well as leftovers

Legend:

- Works with both Boxed and Homemade Mac & Cheese
- Works with Homemade Mac & Cheese only
- 15 minutes
- 30 minutes
- 45 minutes
- 1 hour
- More than 1 hour
- Vegetarian
- Contains meat, poultry or fish
- Often liked by kids
- Good for entertaining
- Works well as leftovers

Quick Hits for Packaged Mac & Cheese

	Page	Boxed/ Homemade	Time	Vegetarian/ Meat	Kids Specials	Good For Company	Good For Leftovers
Meatballs	27	box	clock	meat	kid		leftovers
Tuna	27	box	clock	meat			leftovers
Ham	27	box	clock	meat	kid		leftovers
Sausage	27	box	clock	meat	kid		leftovers
Hot dogs	27	box	clock	meat	kid		leftovers
Hamburger	27	box	clock	meat	kid		leftovers
Chicken	27	box	clock	meat	kid		leftovers
Green chilies	28	box	clock	veg			leftovers
Zucchini	28	box	clock	veg			leftovers
Mushrooms	28	box	clock	veg			leftovers
Green peppers	28	box	clock	veg			leftovers
Peas	28	box	clock	veg			leftovers
Broccoli	28	box	clock	veg			leftovers
Sundried tomatoes	28	box	clock	veg			leftovers
Fresh tomatoes	28	box	clock	veg			leftovers
Corn	29	box	clock	veg	kid		leftovers
Spinach	29	box	clock	veg			
Red bell peppers	29	box	clock	veg			leftovers
Black beans and salsa	29	box	clock	veg			
Mixed vegetables	29	box	clock	veg			leftovers
Green beans	29	box	clock	veg			leftovers
Cabbage	29	box	clock	veg			leftovers
Asparagus	29	box	clock	veg			leftovers
Olives	29	box	clock	veg			leftovers
Kiwi	30	box	clock	veg			
Raisins	30	box	clock	veg			
Fresh apples	30	box	clock	veg			
Cinnamon apples	30	box	clock	veg			
Pears	30	box	clock	veg			
Cashews	31	box	clock	veg			leftovers
Goldfish®	31	box	clock	veg	kid		
Cheese baked rolls	31	box	clock	veg	kid		leftovers
Stuffing	31	box	clock	veg	kid		leftovers
Walnuts	31	box	clock	veg			leftovers
French fried onion rings	31	box	clock	veg			
Honey roasted peanuts	31	box	clock	veg			leftovers
Risotto	32	box	clock (half)	veg			
Gnocchi	32	box	clock	veg			
Deli fried	33	homemade	clock	veg			
Chili	34	box	clock	meat	kid		leftovers

	Page	Boxed/ Homemade	Time	Vegetarian/ Meat	Kids Specials	Good For Company	Good For Leftovers
Bacon, tomato and Cheddar	36	Boxed	◑	Meat			Leftovers
Baked fettuccine	37	Homemade	●+	Meat		Company	Leftovers
Baked rigatoni	38	Homemade	●+	Vegetarian		Company	Leftovers
Beef and veggie casserole	40	Boxed	●	Meat			Leftovers
Beef pot pie	41	Boxed	●	Meat	Kids	Company	
Beef stroganoff	42	Boxed	●	Meat		Company	Leftovers
Broccoli cheese casserole	43	Boxed	●	Vegetarian		Company	
Carbonara (bacon and Parmesan)	44	Boxed	◑	Meat			
Cheeseburger pie	45	Boxed	◕	Meat	Kids		Leftovers
Cheesy pasta	46	Homemade	◑	Vegetarian	Kids	Company	
Favorite tomato sauce	46	Homemade	◑	Vegetarian		Company	Leftovers
Cream of mushroom mac & cheese	47	Boxed	◔	Vegetarian			Leftovers
Creole-style	48	Boxed	◔	Meat			Leftovers
French onion mac & cheese	49	Homemade	●	Vegetarian		Company	
Green chili and chicken	50	Boxed	◑	Meat			Leftovers
Grilled mac & cheese sandwich	51	Boxed	◑	Meat	Kids		
Mac & cheese low fat special	52	Boxed	◕	Vegetarian			Leftovers
Mac & cheese fiesta	53	Boxed	◔	Meat	Kids		Leftovers
Meatballs - Mexican	54	Boxed	●	Meat			Leftovers
Meatballs - Swedish	55	Boxed	◕	Meat	Kids		Leftovers
Mega lasagna	56	Homemade	●+	Vegetarian			Leftovers
Paella	58	Boxed	●	Meat			
Pepper steak	59	Boxed	●	Meat			Leftovers
Pizza	60	Homemade	●	Meat	Kids	Company	Leftovers
Primavera	63	Boxed	◑	Vegetarian		Company	
Prosciutto and peas	64	Boxed	◔	Meat			Leftovers
Sausage, red peppers and corn	65	Boxed	◑	Meat			Leftovers
Shepherd's pie	66	Boxed	●+	Meat		Company	Leftovers
Sloppy corn checkerboard	67	Boxed	◕	Meat	Kids		Leftovers
Sloppy joes	68	Boxed	◑	Meat	Kids		
Southwest	69	Boxed	◔	Vegetarian			Leftovers
Stuffed bell peppers	70	Boxed	●	Meat		Company	
Tomatoes, olives and goat cheese	72	Boxed	◑	Vegetarian		Company	
Tuna casserole	73	Boxed	◕	Meat	Kids		Leftovers
Turkey casserole	74	Boxed	●	Meat		Company	Leftovers
Wild mushrooms	75	Boxed	◑	Vegetarian		Company	Leftovers
Zucchini, basil and Parmesan	76	Boxed	◔	Vegetarian		Company	

Appetizers, Sides & Salads

	Page	Boxed/ Homemade	Time	Vegetarian/ Meat	Kids Specials	Good For Company	Good For Leftovers
Mac & cheese balls with marinara sauce	81	Both	More than 1 hour	Vegetarian	Kids		Leftovers
Broccoli with Gorgonzola shells	82	Homemade only	30 minutes	Vegetarian		Company	
Cobb salad	83	Both	More than 1 hour	Meat			
Corn mac custards with roasted red pepper sauce	84	Both	1 hour	Vegetarian		Company	
Deviled eggs	78	Both	45 minutes	Vegetarian			Leftovers
Ham & cheese roll-ups	79	Both	More than 1 hour	Meat	Kids		Leftovers
Parmesan, olive and pepper pasta salad	85	Homemade only	30 minutes	Vegetarian			Leftovers
Pot stickers	86	Both	1 hour	Meat		Company	
Ratatouille	87	Both	30 minutes	Vegetarian		Company	Leftovers
Rotolino	88	Homemade only	More than 1 hour	Vegetarian		Company	Leftovers
Salad with Roquefort, pears and pecans	90	Homemade only	45 minutes	Vegetarian		Company	
Salami macaroni canapés	79	Both	45 minutes	Meat			
Squash filled with mac & cheese	91	Both	More than 1 hour	Vegetarian			
Stuffed baked potatoes	92	Both	1 hour	Meat	Kids		Leftovers
Stuffed mushrooms	94	Both	45 minutes	Vegetarian		Company	Leftovers
Stuffed pasilla peppers	95	Both	30 minutes	Vegetarian		Company	
Tuna macaroni salad	96	Both	30 minutes	Meat	Kids		Leftovers

Mac & Cheese Beginnings and Endings

	Page	Boxed/ Homemade	Time	Vegetarian/ Meat	Kids Specials	Good For Company	Good For Leftovers
Frittata	98	Both	45 minutes	Vegetarian			
Ham and eggs	99	Both	30 minutes	Meat	Kids		
Jam tarts	102	Homemade only	More than 1 hour	Vegetarian	Kids		Leftovers
Apple crisp	103	Both	More than 1 hour	Vegetarian	Kids		Leftovers
Honey pepper feta bake	104	Homemade only	30 minutes	Vegetarian		Company	

Legend:

- Works with both Boxed and Homemade Mac & Cheese
- Works with Homemade Mac & Cheese only
- 15 minutes
- 30 minutes
- 45 minutes
- 1 hour
- More than 1 hour
- Vegetarian
- Contains meat, poultry or fish
- Often liked by kids
- Good for entertaining
- Works well as leftovers

Visit **www.maccheese.com** for the inside story.

Introduction

Top 10 Reasons To Eat Mac & Cheese

10. Tastes great!

9. Easy to make!

8. Kids love it!

7. Cheap!

6. Fast!

5. Is a meal in itself!

4. Has as few as 2 ingredients!

3. Anyone can make it!

2. Everyone will like you!

1. You can make all the great recipes in this book!

REJECTED You can eat it without any teeth

REJECTED Protects your fall if you nod off at the dinner table

REJECTED You can tell small children it's yellow candy

If you hold it to your ears you can hear the wind rustling through the cheese fields

Ideal for that new Pasta and Cheddar Diet Plan

Grows mold very slowly

REJECTED Even if it clogs your arteries, the blood can flow through the little tubes

REJECTED Cheaper than Prozac

REJECTED Comes in convenient nostril sizes

Doesn't taste like brussel sprouts

REJECTED

Visit **www.maccheese.com** to see all the rejected reasons.

Chapter 1

When You've Got the Time,
Think Outside the Box:

HOMEMADE
Mac & Cheese

Homemade Mac & Cheese Overview

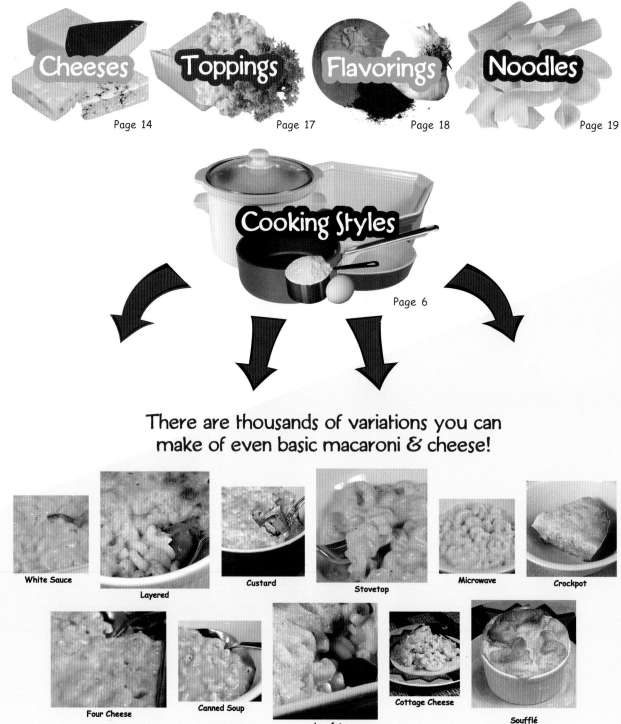

Cheeses — Page 14

Toppings — Page 17

Flavorings — Page 18

Noodles — Page 19

Cooking Styles — Page 6

There are thousands of variations you can make of even basic macaroni & cheese!

White Sauce

Layered

Custard

Stovetop

Microwave

Crockpot

Four Cheese

Canned Soup

Low fat

Cottage Cheese

Soufflé

Tips that apply to all the recipes...

Types of Milk

Fat free milk = not the best unless you're counting calories
2% milk = noticeably more taste and color than skim milk
Whole milk = richer than 2%, but not a big difference
Evaporated milk = richer still, with a silky smooth texture

Useful Conversions

8 oz. of dried elbow macaroni = 1 3/4 cup
4 oz. of shredded cheese = 1 cup

Tips for all the baked recipes...

Baking Dishes

Shallower baking dishes	Deeper baking dishes
Faster evaporation	Slower evaporation
Sauce becomes thicker	Sauce stays creamier
Larger surface for toppings	Smaller surface for toppings

Baking Times

Shorter baking time	Longer baking time
Sauce stays creamier	Sauce becomes thicker
Less browning on surface	More browning on surface

Comparison - 11 Different Cooking Styles

	Name	Description	Easy?	Time?
	1. White sauce	This is the most common style of mac & cheese. It starts with a basic white sauce, and is baked in the oven.	Medium	1 hour
	2. Layered	This is a simple baked mac & cheese, where macaroni and cheese are layered in the baking dish.	Easy	1 hour
	3. Custard	Another baked mac & cheese, with a milk and egg custard poured over the dish.	Easy	1 hour
	4. Stovetop	No baking for this one - it's all done on the stovetop.	Medium	30 min
	5. Microwave	No baking here either - most of the cooking is done in the microwave.	Easy	30 min
	6. Crockpot	If you've got a slow cooker, this is very easy, but takes a lot of time.	Easiest	5 hours
	7. Four cheese	A rich and creamy version, using four different cheeses.	Medium	1 hour
	8. Canned soup	A short-cut version, using canned Cheddar cheese soup.	Easy	45 min
	9. Low fat	Mac & cheese is normally not a low fat dish, but here's a version that cuts way down on fat and calories.	Medium	1 hour
	10. Cottage cheese	Cottage cheese is used in this one to lighten it up.	Easy	1 hour
	11. Soufflé	Light and airy, this soufflé version has a very different consistency than the others.	Most difficult	1 hour

Taste	Texture	Cal. / From Fat	Tasting Notes
Rich flavor, but can be pasty if roux is not cooked enough.	Thick cheesy sauce that coats your mouth.	481 / 229	The classic dish. Good if you're looking for the thick, saucy kind of mac & cheese.
Simple flavors stand out, not mixed with sauce.	Not creamy. No sauce, just noodles and cheese.	411 / 181	Although largely the same ingredients as the white sauce version, it seems lighter, not filling your mouth the same way.
Good cheese flavor.	Firmer texture, holds together more than others.	471/ 210	This also seems lighter than the white sauce version, although calories are about the same.
Good cheese flavor.	Thick, cheesy sauce, very smooth.	548/ 277	Very creamy and smooth, with rich taste and feel. You lose the option for a baked, browned topping, though.
Good cheese flavor.	Creamy and smooth.	466/ 223	Surprisingly good. A real contender, though it also misses out on the baked toppings.
Good cheese flavor.	Firm, not saucy. Holds together.	550/ 252	Easiest to prepare, but long cooking time. Custard-type, gives a result that's firm enough to serve in wedges.
Combined cheeses give rich, complex flavor.	Like white sauce version, but cheeses used can alter the texture.	536/ 244	Very rich, and the multiple cheeses give an interesting, complex flavor. You can vary it to suit your tastes by using different combinations.
Cheesy enough, but also a bit salty.	Slightly grainy.	407/ 173	Easy to make and has plenty of cheese flavor, though it could be too salty for some people.
Mild - could use added flavoring.	Thick, doesn't feel low fat.	277/ 81	This version works surprisingly well. Not as thick or rich as some of the others, but certainly acceptable.
Bland - needs some added flavoring.	Lighter texture, non-grainy.	508/ 240	Lighter taste and feel, but not actually lighter on calories. Could use something added to liven up the flavor.
Less dense, so flavor seems lighter.	Very light and puffy.	173/ 74	Light , airy and elegant - not as heavy and filling as others. But it's more work, and might not seem like "real" mac & cheese.

** Cal. / From fat column shows calories per serving, and calories from fat per serving.

The Basic Recipes

These basic recipes don't include special flavorings or toppings, and mostly just call for Cheddar cheese. You can start with any of these recipes as a base, then vary it as described later in the chapter. Mix and match to your heart's content!

1. White Sauce

This is what most people think of as classic mac & cheese - thick, rich and saucy.

Serves 4 to 6

8 oz. dried elbow macaroni
2 tbsp. butter
2 tbsp. flour
1 1/2 c. milk
2 1/2 c. (10 oz.) sharp Cheddar, shredded
Salt and pepper

» Preheat oven to 350 degrees.
» Cook macaroni in boiling, salted water, until al dente. Drain.
» In a saucepan, melt butter over Medium-low heat.
» When butter is melted, stir in flour to make a roux. Cook, whisking constantly, 3 minutes.
» Add milk slowly in a stream, while whisking.
» Cook milk sauce, whisking, until slightly thickened.
» Stir cheese into sauce until thoroughly combined and melted.
» Stir macaroni into sauce. Season with salt and pepper to taste.
» Spray baking dish with non-stick spray.
» Transfer macaroni and cheese to baking dish, spreading evenly.
» Bake 25 to 30 minutes, or until cheese is bubbly.

2. Layered

This is a simple, straight-forward approach to baked macaroni & cheese.

Serves 4 to 6

8 oz. dried elbow macaroni
2 1/2 c. (10 oz.) sharp Cheddar, shredded
Salt and pepper
3/4 c. milk

» Preheat oven to 350 degrees.
» Cook macaroni in boiling, salted water, until al dente. Drain.
» Spray casserole dish with non-stick spray.
» Put 1/3 of the macaroni in the casserole dish. Cover with 1/3 of the cheese. Season with salt and pepper.
» Add two more layers the same way.
» Pour milk evenly over the top of the dish.
» Bake uncovered, 30 to 40 minutes, or until milk is no longer liquid, and surface begins to brown.
» Let stand 5 minutes before serving.

1 hour

3. Custard

This version uses eggs, has a firmer texture, and doesn't feel quite so rich.

Serves 4 to 6

8 oz. dried elbow macaroni
2 1/2 c. (10 oz.) sharp Cheddar, shredded
Salt and pepper
2 eggs
1 1/2 c. milk

» Preheat oven to 350 degrees.
» Cook macaroni in boiling, salted water, until al dente. Drain.
» Combine macaroni and cheese in a large bowl.
» Season macaroni with salt and pepper to taste.
» Spray baking dish with non-stick spray.
» Place macaroni mixture in baking dish, patting down evenly.
» Beat eggs together with milk.
» Pour milk mixture evenly over macaroni.
» Bake 35 to 40 minutes, or until bubbly and top begins to brown.

30 minutes

4. Stove Top

This version is fast (no baking), and has a very smooth and creamy texture.

Serves 4 to 6

8 oz. dried elbow macaroni
2 tbsp. butter
1 1/4 c. (10 oz.) evaporated milk
2 large eggs, beaten
2 1/2 c. (10 oz.) sharp Cheddar, shredded
Salt and pepper

» Cook macaroni in boiling, salted water, until al dente. Drain.
» Return macaroni to pan, and toss with butter until melted.
» Beat together milk and eggs. Pour into a large saucepan, and put on Medium-low heat.
» Stir half of cheese into milk. Cook, whisking, until cheese is melted and mixture is smooth.
» Add macaroni and rest of cheese. Cook, stirring frequently, until cheese is melted and sauce is creamy.
» Season with salt and pepper, and serve immediately.

5. Microwave

This recipe makes a creamy dish, that's faster than any of the baked versions.

Serves 4 to 6

8 oz. dried elbow macaroni
1 1/4 c. milk
1 tbsp. + 1 tsp. cornstarch
2 tbsp. butter, cut into bits
1 1/2 c. (6 oz.) sharp Cheddar, shredded
4 oz. American cheese, shredded or cut into bits
Salt and pepper

» Cook macaroni in boiling, salted water, until al dente. Drain.
» In a microwave-safe covered dish, whisk together milk and cornstarch.
» Stir butter, half the Cheddar, and half the American cheese into milk.
» Cover, and microwave on Medium (50%) for 5 minutes.
» Whisk milk mixture until smooth.
» Stir in remaining cheeses, mix thoroughly, then stir in macaroni.
» Season with salt and pepper to taste.
» Cover, and microwave on Medium another 6 minutes, stirring halfway through.
» Give macaroni a final stir, then let it stand for 5 minutes before serving.

6. Crockpot

This recipe takes all day, but don't worry! It's very easy, and requires minimal active time.

Serves 4 to 6

2 eggs, beaten lightly
1 1/2 c. milk
1 can (12 oz.) evaporated milk
2 1/2 c. (10 oz.) sharp Cheddar, shredded
8 oz. dried elbow macaroni
Salt and pepper

» In a large bowl, mix eggs, milk, and evaporated milk, combining thoroughly.
» Reserve 1/2 c. shredded cheese. Stir remaining 2 c. cheese and macaroni into milk mixture.
» Season mixture with salt and pepper to taste.
» Spray inside of crockpot with non-stick spray.
» Pour macaroni mixture into crockpot.
» Sprinkle reserved cheese on top.
» Cook on Low heat for 5 hours, or until edges are beginning to brown. Leave it alone as it cooks – don't open the lid or stir.

7. Four Cheese

1 hour

"This decadently rich version of macaroni and cheese is worth every bit of the effort of making it from scratch." - Maryann Murtha, Malverne, NY

Serves 4 to 6

8 oz. dried elbow macaroni
2 tbsp. butter
2 tbsp. flour
1 can (12 oz.) evaporated milk
1/2 c. milk (2% or whole milk, not fat free)
3/4 c. (3 oz.) Vermont white Cheddar, shredded
3/4 c. (3 oz.) Gouda, shredded
3/4 c. (3 oz.) Pecorino Romano, shredded
1/4 c. (1 oz.) Asiago, shredded
Salt and pepper

» Preheat oven to 350 degrees.
» Cook macaroni in boiling, salted water, until al dente. Drain.
» In a saucepan, melt butter over Medium-low heat.
» When butter is melted, stir in flour to make a roux. Cook, whisking constantly, 3 minutes.
» Add evaporated and regular milk slowly in a stream, while whisking.
» Cook milk sauce, whisking, until slightly thickened.
» Add first three cheeses to sauce. Stir cheese into sauce until thoroughly combined and melted.
» Stir macaroni into sauce. Season with salt and pepper to taste.
» Spray baking dish with non-stick spray.
» Transfer macaroni and cheese to a baking dish, spreading evenly.
» Sprinkle Asiago cheese over top.
» Bake 25 to 30 minutes, or until cheese is bubbly.

8. Canned Soup

45 minutes

Easy on the shaker, because this version is pretty salty even without adding any salt.

Serves 4 to 6

8 oz. dried elbow macaroni
3/4 c. canned condensed Cheddar cheese soup
1/2 c. milk
2 c. (8 oz.) sharp Cheddar, shredded
Pepper (and salt if desired)

» Preheat oven to 350 degrees.
» Cook macaroni in boiling, salted water, until al dente. Drain.
» Return macaroni to the pan. Stir in soup, milk, and Cheddar cheese, until mixed well.
» Season with pepper. Add salt if desired.
» Spray baking dish with non-stick spray, and fill with macaroni mixture, patting down evenly.
» Bake 25 to 30 minutes, or until cheese is brown and bubbly.

9. Low Fat

1 hour

Finally, a low fat macaroni & cheese with good texture and taste! Use a deep baking dish to keep it creamy.

Serves 6 (277 calories per serving)

8 oz. dried elbow macaroni
2 tbsp. low fat margarine
2 tbsp. flour
1 1/2 c. skim milk
3/4 c. (3 oz.) low fat Cheddar, shredded
3 slices (2 oz.) low fat American cheese, cut into bits
2 oz. light cream cheese, cut into bits
Salt and pepper
1.5 tbsp. grated Parmesan

» Preheat oven to 350 degrees.
» Cook macaroni in boiling, salted water, until al dente. Drain.
» In a saucepan, melt margarine over Medium-low heat.
» When margarine is melted, stir in flour to make a roux. Cook, whisking constantly, 3 minutes.
» Add milk slowly in a stream, while whisking.
» Cook milk sauce, whisking, until slightly thickened.
» Add first three cheeses to sauce. Stir cheese into sauce until completely melted.
» Stir macaroni into sauce. Season with salt and pepper to taste.
» Spray baking dish with non-stick spray.
» Transfer macaroni and cheese to baking dish, patting down evenly.
» Sprinkle top with Parmesan.
» Bake 25 to 30 minutes, or until cheese is bubbly.

10. Cottage Cheese

1 hour

This recipe has a lighter texture and taste. Try it with with one or more of the optional flavorings and toppings.

Serves 4 to 6

8 oz. dried elbow macaroni
1 egg
2 c. cottage cheese
1 c. sour cream
1 1/2 c. (6 oz.) sharp Cheddar, shredded
Salt and pepper

» Preheat oven to 350 degrees.
» Cook macaroni in boiling, salted water, until al dente. Drain.
» In a large bowl, beat egg lightly.
» Add cottage cheese, sour cream, and Cheddar to the bowl, and mix well.
» Add macaroni to bowl, and mix well.
» Season with salt and pepper to taste.
» Spray baking dish with non-stick spray.
» Place macaroni mixture in baking dish, patting down evenly.
» Bake 30-40 minutes, or until bubbly and top begins to brown.

1 hour

11. Soufflé

Think mac & cheese is heavy? Think again! Serve with a salad, for a light and elegant lunch.

Makes 8 individual soufflés.

4 oz. dried elbow macaroni
3 large eggs
1 1/3 c. milk
1 1/2 c. (6 oz.) sharp Cheddar, shredded
1 c. soft breadcrumbs (one slice bread)
Salt and pepper
1/4 tsp. cream of tartar

» Preheat oven to 375 degrees.
» Cook macaroni in boiling, salted water, until al dente. Drain.
» While macaroni is cooking, separate eggs, keeping both yolks and whites.
» Beat yolks lightly, then combine with milk in a small saucepan.
» Cook milk over Medium heat, whisking occasionally, until thickened slightly.
» Remove milk from heat, and add cheese. Stir until cheese is melted.
» Add breadcrumbs and macaroni to cheese, and mix well.
» Season macaroni mixture with salt and pepper to taste.
» Beat egg whites with cream of tartar until stiff but not dry.
» Whisk one quarter of whites into macaroni, then carefully fold in the remaining whites, gently but thoroughly.
» Spray individual soufflé dishes with non-stick spray.
» Fill soufflé dishes almost to the top with macaroni mixture, and smooth the surface.
» Bake 15 to 20 minutes, or until top is well puffed up and golden brown.
» Serve immediately.

Comparison · A World of Cheeses

Cheddar is the classic for mac & cheese, but it's certainly not the only choice!

Name	Taste	Taste Stands Alone?	Texture	Tasting Notes
American	Mild cheesy flavor	Yes, but additions optional	Very smooth, melts well	Another classic taste. Not as much flavor as Cheddar, but smoother texture.
Asiago	Rich, nutty, with a tang	Yes, or blend with others	Fairly smooth	Rich flavor could be too much by itself, but great for mixing with other cheeses.
Boursin®	Lots of flavor, garlic & herbs	Yes. Don't add anything	Smooth	Great as a side dish, but probably too rich for a full dinner.
Brie	Distinctive, not too strong	Yes. Don't add anything	Ultra creamy	Good if you like the taste of Brie. Probably best for adults.
Canned cheese spread	Not much	No	Thin	Thin in all respects. Not recommended.
Cheddar (sharp yellow)	Classic, full flavor	Yes, but additions optional	Can be grainy	The classic mac flavor. Dish is more colorful than with white cheeses.
Cheddar (Vermont white)	Classic, very rich	Yes, but additions optional	Creamy	Better texture (less grainy) than sharp yellow Cheddar.
Chèvre (goat cheese)	Mild, but distinctive	Best with additions	Very smooth	Smooth, and a good foundation for other flavors. Probably best for adults.
Cream cheese	Very little	No. Add flavorings	Smooth	Texture is good, but little taste. Could use it with other cheeses, but doesn't work well by itself.
Emmental	Swiss flavor, milder than Gruyère	Yes, but additions optional	Not very creamy, somewhat stringy	Good Swiss flavor. Very buttery, leaves pool at bottom of dish.
Feta	Fairly sharp, tangy	Yes, but additions optional	Smooth	Very distinctive and flavorful. Try as a side dish with other Mediterranean flavors.
Fontina	Mild & pleasant	Best with additions	Smooth	Mild, unobjectionable flavor goes well with added flavorings or mixed with other cheeses.
Gorgonzola	Strong blue cheese flavor	Yes. Don't add anything	Creamy	Works well as a side dish, for people who like blue cheese. Too much for a main course. Other blue cheeses would work, too.

Name	Taste	Taste Stands Alone?	Texture	Tasting Notes
Gouda	Smooth, not strong	Yes, but additions optional	Smooth, not grainy or stringy	Nice flavor and texture, overall smoothness.
Gruyère	Sharp flavor, like cheese fondue	Yes, or blend with others	Cheese is very thick	Strong flavor could be cut by mixing with milder cheese.
Havarti	Very smooth & mild	Best with additions	Creamy	Mild, smooth flavor. Buttery, leaves pool at bottom of dish.
Jack	Bland	No. Add flavorings	Smooth, non-grainy	Not much flavor by itself, but goes well with other cheeses or flavorings.
Mozzarella	Very bland	No	Stringy and thin	Little flavor and unusual texture. Not recommended, except for kids who like stringy cheese.
Muenster	Medium-mild flavor, not too strong	Yes, but additions optional	Thick and smooth	Works by itself, but would go well with other flavorings, too.
Pecorino Romano	Full flavor, fairly sharp	Yes, but additions optional	A bit thin, not as smooth as some	Very full flavored, really stands out. Works well combined with milder cheeses too.
Pepper Jack	Hot & spicy - strong pepper taste	Yes, or blend with others	Smooth	Not a lot of cheese flavor, but plenty of pepper. Too much for a main course, but mix with another cheese, or use as a side dish.
Port wine cheese spread	Odd taste, a bit alcoholic	No	A bit sticky	Very strange. Not recommended.
Provolone	Very mild	No. Add flavorings	Stringy, but not as thin as Mozzarella	Not much flavor on its own, but could mix with another cheese or add flavorings.
Ricotta	No flavor	No	Gritty	Not recommended.
Swiss (standard American pkg.)	Milder than Gruyère or Emmental	Yes, but additions optional	Smooth	Smoother consistency and milder flavor than Emmental or Gruyère.
Velveeta	Full flavor, similar to American	Yes, but additions optional	Smooth, but sticks to your mouth and teeth	Melts well and has lots of flavor, but very sticky to eat. You may love it or hate it.
Wisconsin farmer's cheese	Very mild	No. Add flavorings	Smooth	Not much flavor, but could combine well with other cheeses.

Mac & Cheese and Celebrities

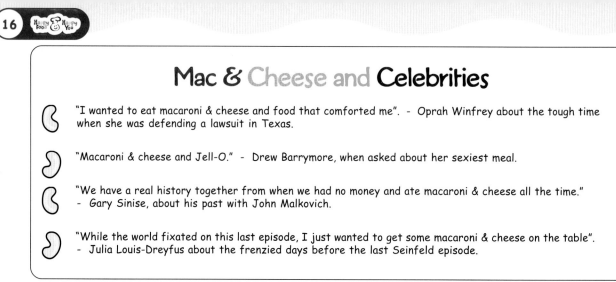

"I wanted to eat macaroni & cheese and food that comforted me". - Oprah Winfrey about the tough time when she was defending a lawsuit in Texas.

"Macaroni & cheese and Jell-O." - Drew Barrymore, when asked about her sexiest meal.

"We have a real history together from when we had no money and ate macaroni & cheese all the time." - Gary Sinise, about his past with John Malkovich.

"While the world fixated on this last episode, I just wanted to get some macaroni & cheese on the table". - Julia Louis-Dreyfus about the frenzied days before the last Seinfeld episode.

HOW WILL THEY SURVIVE NOW?

Comparison - What Goes On Top

For baked mac & cheese, you can add any of the following toppings before putting it into the oven. For non-baked versions, you could top each serving with one of these, although you won't get the same oven-browned effect.

	Name	Directions	Tasting Notes
	Breadcrumbs (plain)	Just sprinkle on top.	Adds some crunch, but no flavor.
	Breadcrumbs (buttered)	Melt butter and stir together with breadcrumbs before putting on top.	Browns better than plain crumbs, still not much taste.
	Breadcrumbs (Italian flavor)	Just sprinkle on top, or you could mix with melted butter first.	Adds quite a bit of flavor. Try with Parmesan too.
	Crushed Doritos	Crush Doritos, then sprinkle on top.	Quite flavorful, adds more crunch than potato chips.
	Crushed potato chips	Crush chips, then sprinkle on top.	Adds a bit of crunch and saltiness. Flavor depends on what type of chips you use.
	Crushed saltines	Crush saltines then sprinkle on top, or mix with melted butter first.	Adds saltiness and texture. Browns best if buttered first.
	Extra cheese (same kind as in mac & cheese)	Sprinkle extra shredded cheese on top.	Adds extra cheese flavor. Cheddar can be a bit grainy.
	Mustard	Spread a very thin layer of mustard (from a jar, not dried mustard) on top of mac & cheese before baking.	Adds a lot of flavor - be careful not to use too much. Could mix with breadcrumbs too.
	Paprika	Sprinkle lightly on top.	Adds a lot of color, and some mild flavor.
	Parmesan cheese	Grate fresh, or use pre-grated. Just sprinkle on top.	Adds some cheesiness, but not a strong flavor.
	Parmesan mixed with buttered breadcrumbs	Stir equal parts breadcrumbs and grated Parmesan together with melted butter, then sprinkle on top of dish.	Combines a bit of cheesiness with crunch and color.
	Parsley	Sprinkle minced parsley on top.	Bright color, a small amount of flavor.
	Pepperoni	Scatter slices of pepperoni over top of dish.	Gives dish an entirely different, pizza-like, flavor.
	Pesto sauce	Spread a thin layer of pesto sauce over top of mac & cheese.	Fresh basil flavor adds an interesting twist. A little goes a long way.
	Stuffing (from mix)	Prepare stuffing according to box directions, and spread about 1/2" layer on top of mac & cheese.	Adds a lot of flavor, works surprisingly well.
	Walnuts	Chop walnuts finely, then sprinkle on top.	Nutty flavor goes well with some cheeses.

Comparison - Spice It Up

You may want to add one (or more) of these ingredients for added flavor. Amounts given here are for a standard size recipe.
»   For baked macaroni & cheese recipes, stir ingredient into the mac & cheese before placing it in the baking dish.
»   For non-baked macaroni & cheese, stir ingredient into the mac & cheese right before serving.

Name	Directions	Tasting Notes
Cayenne pepper	Mix 1/8 tsp. cayenne pepper into macaroni & cheese.	Nice touch of flavor. You can add more kick by increasing the amount.
Celery	Chop 2 stalks of celery. Sauté in butter until just softened, then stir into mac & cheese.	Pleasant, mild flavor, and a bit of a crunch. Works well with onions too, or if you're using stuffing as a topping.
Garlic	Mince 2 small cloves garlic. Sauté garlic in butter, then add to mac & cheese. Or, you could use garlic powder instead.	Lots of flavor in a small amount. Good if you like garlic.
Horseradish	Stir 1 tsp. prepared horseradish into macaroni & cheese.	Adds tang, works well with Cheddar. Careful - this is not a subtle flavor, and could overpower the rest of the dish.
Mace	Stir a scant 1/8 tsp. ground mace into macaroni & cheese.	Interesting, unusual flavor. Strong stuff, you only need a little.
Mustard (Dijon, or your favorite)	Mix 2 tsp. mustard into the macaroni & cheese.	Adds complexity to the flavor. With milder cheeses, go easy on the mustard.
Mustard (dried)	Mix 1 tsp. into macaroni & cheese.	Similar to Dijon, but sharper and less rounded flavor.
Nutmeg	Mix 1/8 tsp. ground nutmeg into macaroni & cheese.	Mild and smooth, adds just a touch of spice.
Onions (sautéed)	Dice 1/2 medium onion. Sauté in butter until soft, then stir into macaroni & cheese. Or, you could use dried, minced onion instead.	Sautéing brings out the sweetness in the onion, adds a pleasant flavor.
Paprika	Mix 1/2 tsp. paprika into the macaroni & cheese.	Mild, subtle flavor. Also deepens the color of the dish. Can be used as a topping instead of being mixed in.
Red wine	Boil 1 c. red wine until alcohol evaporated, and reduced by about two thirds. Stir into macaroni & cheese.	Tastes pretty good, but you have to get past the odd, purplish color of the dish.
Tabasco® sauce	Mix 1/8 tsp. Tabasco® into the macaroni & cheese. Add more if needed to get desired level of heat.	Adds both flavor and some bite, depending on how much you use.
Tomatoes (canned)	Drain 1 can (14.5 oz.) diced, stewed tomatoes. Stir into macaroni & cheese.	Works well, but it's a big change. Tomatoes come to the forefront, and it tastes like a very different dish.
Worcestershire sauce	Mix 1 1/4 tsp. Worcestershire into the macaroni & cheese.	Small amount fills out the flavor nicely, but potent if you use more than this.

Comparison - It's About the Noodles

Why limit yourself to just elbow macaroni? Pasta comes in a huge variety of shapes, and different colors, too. Some of these work better for "macaroni & cheese" than others. We've included a few major types here, and you can experiment further on your own.

	Name	Tasting Notes		Name	Tasting Notes
	Capellini (Angel Hair)	Can hold a lot of sauce - some people like, some don't. Be careful not to overcook.		Orecchiette (little ears)	Small cup shapes hold a bit of sauce, and noodles clump and layer in different ways to provide variety. Can be harder to find than other pastas, but it works well.
	Egg noodles	Slightly different taste than the others. Can hold a lot of sauce - too much for some tasters.		Penne	Works well; good proportion of sauce.
	Elbow macaroni	Works well. Hollow shape allows sauce to get inside too, but not as much as in larger noodles like rigatoni.		Radiatorre	Works well, hold a good amount of sauce with a fairly fine "al dente".
	Farfalle (Bow-ties)	Works well, good sauce proportion. A little difficult to cook well as the ends are not as thick as the "knot".		Rigatoni	Large tubes hold a lot, so that biting into a single noodle can release a big mouthful of sauce. You may or may not like this.
	Fettuccine	Doesn't hold the sauce as well as other shapes, and the noodles start to stick together.		Rotelle (Wagon wheels)	Works well; holds a good amount of sauce.
	Gemelli	Works fairly well; a little lower sauce proportion than others.		Rotini (spirals)	Spiral edges give an interesting texture, and hold a good proportion of sauce. Works well.
	Lasagna	Works best in recipes designed for lasagna.		Small shells	Hold quite a bit of sauce, and work well. Texture doesn't stand out as much as rotini.
	Manicotti	Really only for stuffing.		Spaghetti	Spaghetti strands don't hold the sauce well. It just doesn't seem right.
	Mostaccioli	Holds a lot of sauce, similar to rigatoni.			

Mixing and Matching

Now what? You've got all these options, but where to go from here? Just pick things that sound good, and combine them however you want...

Stovetop recipe
Small shell pasta
1 1/2 c. **Swiss** cheese
1 c. **Muenster**
Add **nutmeg**
Sprinkle with **parsley** when serving

White Sauce recipe
1 3/4 c. sharp **Cheddar**
3/4 c. **Havarti**
Mix in **paprika** and sautéed **onion**
Top with buttered **breadcrumbs**

Our Favorite Mix & Match Version

We've made hundreds of variations on macaroni & cheese, with different cheeses, toppings, flavorings, and noodles. After all this, what's our favorite? It was a tough choice, but here's the combination that won us over.

* White Sauce
* Cheddar + Fontina
* Worcestershire + cayenne pepper
* Buttered Italian breadcrumbs

1 hour

Serves 4 to 6

8 oz. dried elbow macaroni
2 tbsp. butter
2 tbsp. flour
1 1/2 c. milk
1 1/2 c. (6 oz.) sharp Cheddar, shredded
1 c. (4 oz.) Fontina, shredded
1 1/4 tsp. Worcestershire sauce
1/8 tsp. cayenne pepper
Salt and pepper
3 tbsp. Italian breadcrumbs
1 tbsp. butter, melted

» Preheat oven to 350 degrees.

» Cook macaroni in boiling, salted water, until al dente. Drain.

» In a saucepan, melt butter over Medium-low heat.

» When butter is melted, stir in flour to make a roux. Cook, whisking constantly, 3 minutes.

» Add milk slowly in a stream, while whisking.

» Cook milk sauce, whisking, until slightly thickened.

» Stir both cheeses into sauce until thoroughly combined and melted.

» Stir Worcestershire and cayenne into sauce until thoroughly combined.

» Stir macaroni into sauce. Season with salt and pepper to taste.

» Spray baking dish with non-stick spray.

» Transfer macaroni and cheese to baking dish, spreading evenly.

» Mix breadcrumbs with melted butter, then sprinkle on top of dish.

» Bake 25 to 30 minutes, or until cheese is bubbly and crumbs are lightly browned.

Chapter 2

They're Hungry
and You've Got No Time:
Mac & Cheese Packages &
Quick Hits

Quick Tips

Cheesier Taste

» Use brands that use real cheese
» Add Cheddar cheese
» Use an extra packet of cheese (or some portion of it)

Reducing Calories

» Use less, or no butter
» Use margarine instead of butter (check the labels)
» Use non-fat milk

Adding Veggies and Other Things

» Cook separately before adding
» Give them their own seasoning

Thicker Consistency

» Use less, or no milk
» Drain the pasta very well, shaking and tossing it repeatedly
» Add grated Parmesan or other cheese
» Use more than one packet of cheese

Best Pasta Preparation

- » Cook pasta until al dente, not mushy – test by tasting
- » Do not boil too hard – it could damage the pasta
- » Do not add oil to the water
- » Add salt to cooking water, depending on how much salt the cheese mix contains
- » Drain well

Faster Cooking

- » Start with hot water
- » Put a lid on the pot
- » Use no more than the recommended amount of water
- » While the water is heating or pasta is cooking, heat the milk and butter in the microwave till the butter melts (watch it closely!)

Leftovers

- » Liven up leftover mac & cheese by adding some of the quick hits on the following pages.
- » For leftovers that already have added ingredients, reheating works best if they used cooked meat or vegetables. Reheating may not work well for uncooked ingredients.

Quick Hits - Meat

Fast ways to liven up your favorite boxed or frozen mac & cheese.
Particularly recommended: meatballs, hot dogs, sausage, tuna!

Meatballs: Get some frozen meatballs, microwave them, and serve on top.

Ham: Get some cooked ham, dice it, add it. Try some diced pineapple, too.

Tuna: Open a can of tuna, drain, add some optional dill, and stir it in there.

Sausage: Cook your favorite sausage, such as breakfast, chicken, or Italian, and add it into the dish.

Hamburger: Cook up some burger, season it with salt, pepper, maybe some chili powder, and mix it in.

Chicken: Buy a roasted chicken, tear it up, and put it in there. You can also try spicing up the chicken with some seasoning and olive oil or butter. Try salt, pepper, oregano, chili powder.

Hot Dogs: Cook some dogs, cut them up, throw them in there.

Quick Hits - Veggies

Fast ways to liven up your favorite boxed or frozen mac & cheese.
Particularly recommended: the green chilies, mushrooms, zucchini and green peppers.

Green Chilies: Doesn't look so good, in the picture or the bowl, but it tastes really good! Open a can of diced chilies and add some of them in.

Zucchini: Slice a zucchini, sauté it in butter or olive oil, and mix it in. Add some salt and pepper while sautéing.

Mushrooms: Buy some sliced mushrooms, sauté them in butter or olive oil, add some salt and pepper, throw them on top.

Peas: Heat up some frozen peas and mix them in.

Green Peppers: Cut up a green pepper, sauté it in butter or olive oil, add salt and pepper, and mix it in.

Broccoli: Cook the broccoli till tender, add salt and pepper, mix it in.

Sundried Tomatoes: Soak the tomatoes if they're not packed in oil, sop up the oil if they are; chop them up, and mix them in.

Fresh Tomatoes: Cube a tomato and throw it in.

Quick Hits - More Veggies

Fast ways to liven up your favorite boxed or frozen mac & cheese.
Particularly recommended: the spinach, red bell peppers, corn, and green beans.

Olives: Get a can of sliced olives and mix them in.

Spinach: Sauté some spinach in butter or olive oil (with fresh, minced garlic if desired). Add salt and pepper, and mix it in.

Red Bell Peppers: Cut up a red pepper, sauté it in butter or olive oil, add salt and pepper, and mix it in.

Asparagus: Cut up some asparagus, sauté in butter or olive oil, add salt and pepper, mix it in.

Corn: Get some canned or frozen corn, heat it up and mix it in. Salt and pepper optional.

Black Beans and Salsa: Heat up some black beans and mix them in; add your favorite salsa on top.

Cabbage: Cut up some cabbage, sauté in butter or olive oil, add salt and pepper, mix it in.

Green Beans: Get some canned or frozen green beans, heat them up, and mix them in. Salt and pepper optional.

Mixed Vegetables: Get some frozen mixed veggies, heat them up, and mix them in. Salt and pepper optional.

Quick Hits - Fruit

Fast ways to liven up your favorite boxed or frozen mac & cheese.
Particularly recommended: the kiwi and raisins!

Raisins - Really good! Add however many look right to you.

Kiwi - Also really good! Peel some kiwi, cut it up, and mix it in!

Fresh Apples - Peel and cut up an apple and mix it in. Works particularly well with some added Cheddar.

Cinnamon Apples - Peel and cut an apple into cubes; put them in a pan with a little butter, sugar, and cinnamon. Heat them till the apples are a little soft, but not mushy. Add as a topping.

Pears - Peel and cut up a pear and add it in. A traditional take on this would use it in a mac & cheese recipe using blue cheese.

Quick Hits - Other Ideas

Fast ways to liven up your favorite boxed or frozen mac & cheese.
Particularly recommended: the cashews and Goldfish®, and cheese baked rolls.

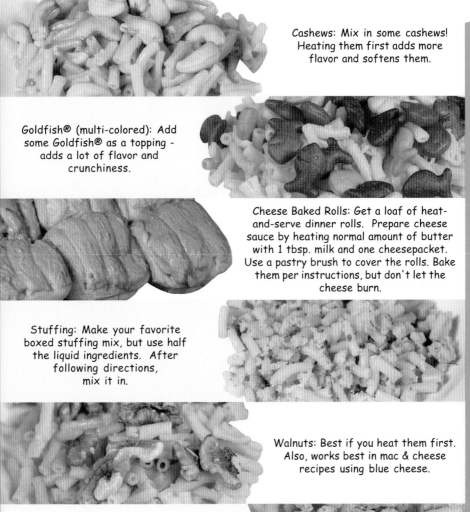

Cashews: Mix in some cashews! Heating them first adds more flavor and softens them.

Goldfish® (multi-colored): Add some Goldfish® as a topping - adds a lot of flavor and crunchiness.

Cheese Baked Rolls: Get a loaf of heat-and-serve dinner rolls. Prepare cheese sauce by heating normal amount of butter with 1 tbsp. milk and one cheesepacket. Use a pastry brush to cover the rolls. Bake them per instructions, but don't let the cheese burn.

Stuffing: Make your favorite boxed stuffing mix, but use half the liquid ingredients. After following directions, mix it in.

Walnuts: Best if you heat them first. Also, works best in mac & cheese recipes using blue cheese.

French Fried Onion Rings: Add as a topping; adds flavor, crunchiness, and (of course) more fat.

Honey Roasted Peanuts: Add as a topping; mostly for those who are already fans.

Quick Hits - Variations on Pasta

Gnocchi

Try using the cheese packet on gnocchi instead of the included pasta.

» Cook a 12-16 ounce package of gnocchi according to the directions.

» Drain the gnocchi, and coat it with a pat or two of butter or margarine, or a tablespoon or two of olive oil.

» Pour in the cheese powder and stir it up.

» Grind some fresh pepper over the top; add some fresh chopped herbs such as basil or parsley too, if you like.

Risotto

You can also try out the cheese powder on risotto.

» Use about one cup of dried Arborio rice.

» Coat the bottom of a pot with olive oil or butter and pour in the rice.

» Stir the rice, attempting to cover all grains with the butter.

» Add 1 3/4 to 2 cups of water, per the package instructions.

» Stirring regularly, cook until most of the water is absorbed and it is soft, but has an al dente center. You may need to add more water to complete the cooking.

» Add the cheese powder and mix it in.

» Grind some fresh pepper over the top; add some fresh chopped herbs such as basil or parsley too, if you like.

Quick Hits - The Easiest
Fried Macaroni & Cheese

This one is so easy it wouldn't count, except that it's so good! Don't you love the taste and feel of those little brown bits in baked macaroni & cheese? Well here's an easy way to get all that you'll ever want!

The number of servings depends on how much you buy.

A container of macaroni & cheese from the deli; start with about half again as much as you want to end up with.

Preparation

» Do not add any oil or butter!

» Bring the mac & cheese to room temperature or warmer using a microwave, if it is not already warm.

» Preheat a large non-stick skillet (the bigger the better) over Medium-high heat.

» Place the mac & cheese in the skillet.

» Spread the mac & cheese around until it's evenly distributed.

» Every minute or so flip the mac & cheese over and stir it up.

» Do not let it burn to black; keep cooking it till you have the amount of brownness you like.

Notes

» For some reason this seems to work best for the kind of mac & cheese you get at deli counters; in the end, it depends of course on the particular kind your deli has – you'll just have to try it!

» Certain homemade recipes and certain frozen brands may also work – generally saucy ones work better; not recommended for boxed mac & cheese.

» This works best if the mac & cheese is already at room temperature or warmer.

» No need to add oil or butter, the cheese should have plenty.

» Make sure you regularly flip over all portions of the mac & cheese, otherwise you'll get pieces burnt to black.

» Remove from the pan as soon as you're done cooking.

» Cooking this way will cause the mac & cheese to reduce in size, so be sure you start with enough.

Quick Hits - The Greatest Chili

15 minutes

Here's a terrific way to spice up your mac & cheese! You can vary it to get just the level of heat you like, and best of all, it takes only minutes to prepare. You'll love this!

Serves 2

1 box macaroni & cheese
1/4 c. milk
1/4 c. margarine
15 oz. can chili
1/4 c. shredded Cheddar cheese (optional)
handful oyster crackers (optional)

"Doesn't get any simpler than this. But you have to actually try it to taste that the whole is greater than the sum of the parts – it surprised me!"

- Debbie K., Prince George, British Columbia

» Prepare macaroni & cheese with milk and margarine according to directions on the box, or your favorite variation.

» While macaroni is cooking, heat chili in a saucepan.

» When macaroni & cheese is ready, scoop macaroni into one side of a bowl, and chili into the other. Repeat for second bowl.

» Scatter Cheddar on top of the bowls, and top chili side with oyster crackers.

Variations

» **Vary spiciness** - Different types of chili vary a lot in ingredients and spiciness, so experiment until you find one that suits you. We preferred chili with beans, but see what you like.

» **Vary proportions** - The basic recipe calls for half mac & cheese, half chili, but you can try macaroni & cheese with just a touch of chili, or vice versa.

» **Make your own chili** - This can be time consuming, but yields the optimal flavor. Whenever you make chili, make a big batch and save some to serve with mac & cheese. It freezes well, so make lots!

When It's Mac & Cheese for
Lunch & Dinner

Macaroni with Bacon, Tomato, and Cheddar

Bacon and tomato add great flavor to this dish.

Serves 3 to 4

1 box macaroni & cheese
1/4 c. milk
1/4 c. margarine
4 strips bacon
Salt and pepper
1 medium tomato, sliced 1/4-inch thick
3/4 c. shredded sharp Cheddar cheese

» Preheat oven to 400 degrees.

» Prepare macaroni & cheese with milk and margarine according to directions on the box, or use your favorite variation.

» While macaroni is cooking, cook bacon in a skillet until crisp but not burned.

» Drain bacon on paper towels, and crumble.

» When macaroni & cheese is prepared, season it with salt and pepper to taste.

» Put macaroni & cheese in a shallow baking dish, patting down evenly.

» Place tomato slices on top of macaroni. Spread shredded cheese on top of dish, then sprinkle with bacon.

» Bake 15 minutes, or until cheese is bubbling.

Baked Fettuccine

This is serious comfort food, with lots of flavor from the sausage and veggies.

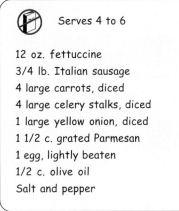

Serves 4 to 6

12 oz. fettuccine
3/4 lb. Italian sausage
4 large carrots, diced
4 large celery stalks, diced
1 large yellow onion, diced
1 1/2 c. grated Parmesan
1 egg, lightly beaten
1/2 c. olive oil
Salt and pepper

Prepare Ingredients
» Preheat oven to 400 degrees.
» The first three main steps, cooking the pasta, sausage, and veggies, can be done at the same time.
» Cook the fettuccine in boiling, salted water until al dente. Drain.
» Coat bottom of empty pot with a little olive oil (not enough to make a pool).
» Return the pasta to the pot, and stir to coat it evenly with the oil. Remove from heat and keep warm.
» If sausage came in links, remove the casings and break sausage up into small chunks.
» Cook sausage over Medium-high heat until well browned.
» Drain sausage in a bowl lined with paper towels.

» Put carrots, celery, and onion in a large skillet and add water to just cover them.
» Boil until the carrots and celery are soft, testing with a fork. Drain vegetables in a colander.
» Sauté vegetables in olive oil until they're lightly browned and have lost most of their moisture.
» Season vegetables with salt and pepper to taste.

Assemble and Bake
» Mix egg into pasta and stir.
» Add Parmesan to pasta and stir well.
» Add sausage and vegetables to pasta. Use two large utensils to repeatedly lift and stir fettuccine until mixed thoroughly.
» Line a 13-inch x 9-inch baking dish with aluminum foil, using enough extra so that it can be folded over double.
» Spray the foil with non-stick spray.
» Pour the fettuccine mixture into the foil, and spread ingredients evenly.
» Wrap foil over the top of pasta and seal, so that mixture is completely enclosed in foil, within the baking dish.
» Bake for 30 minutes. Remove from oven, and let cool for 10 minutes.
» Unwrap foil from top of dish, and invert onto a serving platter. Remove rest of foil.
» Slice to serve.

Baked Rigatoni

This recipe takes some time and effort, but the results are terrific.

Serves 2 to 3

2 green bell peppers

3 c. Favorite Tomato Sauce (p. 46), or other tomato-based pasta sauce

12 oz. dried rigatoni

2 tbsp. olive oil

1/4 c. chopped fresh parsley or basil

8 oz. shredded Fontina cheese

1/2 c. grated Parmesan cheese

1/4 tsp. dried oregano

1/4 tsp. coarse sea salt

Prepare Ingredients

» These first three steps, cooking the peppers, sauce, and rigatoni, can all overlap.

» Turn on broiler. Put peppers on a large piece of aluminum foil, and place under broiler, about 6 inches from heat. Watch them closely to prevent burning.

» Using a kitchen timer, check the peppers every 4 minutes, and turn over each time. Keep cooking and turning until skin is brown or a little black all over (about 16-20 minutes).

» When all sides are brown/black, remove from oven and wrap in foil. Let sit for 5 minutes.

» Pull out stem section. Cut open peppers, and scrape out seeds. Turn over and scrape off most of the skin. Discard stem, seeds, and skin. Dice peppers.

» While the peppers are cooking, make the tomato sauce according to directions on page 46.

» While sauce is simmering, cook the rigatoni in boiling, salted water until al dente.

» Run rigatoni under cold water to stop the cooking, then drain.

ALIEN ENCOUNTERS

(Continued from previous page)

Assemble and Bake

» Preheat oven to 450 degrees.

» Add peppers, olive oil, and parsley or basil to sauce. Stir well.

» Mix rigatoni and sauce, and blend well.

» Place pasta in a large, shallow baking dish, or individual baking dishes. Ideally, the pasta should be only 1 to 2 noodles deep.

» Spread the Fontina cheese over the pasta.

» Sprinkle Parmesan over the pasta, then sprinkle on the oregano.

» Sprinkle top lightly with coarse sea salt.

» Bake 20 to 30 minutes, until cheese is golden brown and bubbly.

» Let cool 15 minutes before eating.

Beef and Veggie Casserole

Worcestershire sauce cooked with the ground beef adds great flavor to this casserole dish.

1 hour

Serves 4

1 box macaroni & cheese
1/4 c. milk
1/4 c. margarine
1 lb. lean ground beef
2 tbsp. Worcestershire sauce
Salt and pepper
1 1/2 tbsp. olive oil
1/2 c. diced onion
2 medium cloves garlic, minced or pressed
1/4 c. diced carrot
1/4 c. diced celery
1 large zucchini, halved lengthwise, then sliced crosswise
1/4 lb. mushrooms, sliced
3/4 c. fresh or frozen green beans
1/2 tsp. dried oregano
1/4 tsp. dried thyme
1/2 c. shredded Cheddar cheese
1 tbsp. Italian-flavored dry breadcrumbs

» Preheat oven to 375 degrees.
» Prepare macaroni & cheese with milk and margarine according to directions on the box, or use your favorite variation.
» While macaroni is cooking, brown ground beef in a large skillet, breaking apart into small pieces.
» When beef is no longer pink, add Worcestershire sauce and salt and pepper to taste.
» Continue to cook beef, stirring frequently, until well browned, at least 5 minutes. Drain beef on paper towels.
» While beef is browning, start the vegetables. In a separate skillet, heat oil over Medium heat, and sauté onion, garlic, carrot and celery 5 minutes.
» Add zucchini and mushrooms to vegetables, and sauté another 5 minutes.
» Season vegetables with salt and pepper as they cook.
» Add beans to vegetables, and cook 3 minutes.
» Combine beef mixture, vegetables, and macaroni & cheese.
» Stir in oregano and thyme, mixing thoroughly.
» Season with salt and pepper to taste.
» Put mixture in a casserole dish, smoothing the top.
» Spread Cheddar evenly over casserole, and then sprinkle with breadcrumbs.
» Bake 25 minutes, or until surface begins to brown.

Mac & Cheese Beef Pot Pie

Homemade pot pie has never been so easy! The basic recipe makes 2 individually sized pot pies - enough for 2 big eaters, or 4 smaller appetites. It's not hard - really, it's not!

Serves 2 to 4

2 frozen pie crusts
1 box macaroni & cheese
1/4 c. milk
1/4 c. margarine
19 oz. can chunky beef soup or stew
1 c. shredded Cheddar cheese (optional)

» Preheat oven to 350 degrees.
» Thaw pie crusts 15 minutes.
» Prepare macaroni & cheese with milk and margarine according to directions on the box, or use your favorite variation.
» While macaroni is cooking, heat soup in a saucepan.
» After thawing shells, press each carefully into individual size oven-proof bowl or soufflé pan, smoothing them out and patching any cracks. Cut off excess around edges.
» Pour soup into pie shells.
» Carefully place spoonfuls of macaroni & cheese on top of pies, covering evenly.
» Scatter Cheddar cheese on top of the pie.
» Bake 35 minutes, or until cheese is melted and starting to brown.

Variations

» **Chicken or turkey pot pie** – Substitute a different filling. You can use any thick and chunky style canned soup or stew.

» **Thicker filling** – If you prefer a thicker filling, there are two approaches. A) Boil the soup over low heat to reduce it, stirring occasionally. B) Use a slotted spoon to put the soup chunks into the pie crusts. Cover with as much of the sauce as you like.

» **Family size pot pie** – Use one deep dish pie crust and make a 9-inch pie. Follow rest of recipe as normal.

» **Added top crust** – Use a second frozen pie shell for the top crust. Let it thaw 15 minutes, roll it out flat, place on top of the filled pie, and crimp edges to seal. Cut slits in the top crust, and brush with lightly beaten egg white before baking.

Mac & Cheese Beef Stroganoff

This delicious and hearty dish is perfect for chilly winter evenings.

1 hour

Serves 3

3/4 lb. boneless beef
2 tbsp. flour
Salt and pepper
1 tbsp. vegetable oil
2 tbsp. butter
1/2 c. chopped white onion
1 large garlic clove, minced or pressed
1/4 lb. sliced mushrooms, white or brown
1/4 c. dry red wine
1/2 c. beef broth
1 box macaroni & cheese
1/4 c. milk
1/4 c. margarine
1/4 c. sour cream
1/2 tsp. Worcestershire sauce
1 tbsp. chopped fresh chives

» Cut beef into strips 1/4-inch thick, 1/2-inch wide, and 2-inch long, removing as much fat as possible.
» Season flour with salt and pepper, and dredge beef in flour mixture.
» In a large skillet, heat oil and 1 tbsp. butter over Medium-high heat until hot but not smoking.
» Brown beef, in batches if necessary, transferring to a plate when done.
» Lower temperature to Medium, and add remaining tbsp. butter to skillet.
» Add onion and garlic to skillet, and sauté until softened, stirring regularly.
» Add mushrooms to skillet, and cook, stirring occasionally, until mushrooms have given off their liquid and it has evaporated.
» Add wine and broth to skillet, and bring to a boil.
» Boil 3 minutes, then reduce heat to Low.
» Return beef to pan with any juices from plate.
» Cover pan and simmer 25 minutes, stirring occasionally.
» While stroganoff is simmering, prepare macaroni & cheese with milk and margarine according to directions on the box, or use your favorite variation.

» When macaroni & cheese is done, stir sour cream and Worcestershire sauce into the stroganoff.
» Season stroganoff with salt and pepper to taste. Heat until almost at a boil.
» Divide macaroni among serving plates, and top with stroganoff.
» Sprinkle dishes with fresh chives, and serve.

Broccoli Cheese Casserole

Broccoli blends perfectly with the macaroni & cheese in this terrific dish. This recipe serves 4 as a main dish (perfect with a salad), or 8 as a side dish.

1 hour

Serves 4 to 8

1 box macaroni & cheese
1/4 c. milk
1/4 c. margarine
2 c. broccoli florets
3/4 c. diced onion
1 tbsp. olive oil
3/4 c. shredded Cheddar cheese
Salt and pepper
1 c. milk
2 eggs
2 tbsp. dry breadcrumbs

"Even my husband liked it!"
- Lucy D., California

» Preheat oven to 350 degrees.
» Prepare macaroni & cheese with milk and margarine according to directions on the box, or use your favorite variation.
» While macaroni is cooking, sauté onion in olive oil until softened.
» Add broccoli, onion and 1/2 c. Cheddar to macaroni & cheese, mixing thoroughly. Season with salt and pepper to taste.
» Put mixture in a casserole dish, smoothing the top.
» In a bowl, beat milk and eggs until combined well.
» Pour milk mixture over macaroni.
» Sprinkle top of casserole with remaining 1/4 c. Cheddar and breadcrumbs.
» Bake 40-45 minutes, or until surface turns golden.

Variations

» **Fastest and easiest** - Drop broccoli in the cooking water 2 minutes after macaroni. Drain broccoli and macaroni together, prepare according to box directions, and then proceed with recipe. After stirring in the onions, Cheddar, and seasonings, just eat it directly. Skip the milk, eggs, breadcrumbs and baking. It's all done in 15 minutes!

Mac & Cheese Carbonara
(Bacon and Parmesan)

Here's a mac & cheese take on carbonara, without the traditional raw egg.

Serves 3

1 box macaroni & cheese
3 tbsp. milk
3 tbsp. margarine
1/4 lb. bacon, chopped
1 large clove garlic, minced or pressed
1/4 c. dry white wine
3 tbsp. heavy cream
1/2 c. grated Parmesan cheese
Salt and pepper
2 tsp. minced fresh parsley (optional)

» Prepare the macaroni & cheese according to box directions, but use only 3 tbsp. each of milk and margarine.

» While macaroni is cooking, cook bacon in a skillet over Medium heat, stirring occasionally, until lightly browned.

» Add garlic to skillet, and cook, stirring, 1 minute.

» Add white wine to skillet, and simmer 5 minutes, until reduced slightly.

» Add cream to skillet, and simmer 2 minutes.

» When macaroni has been prepared, add the bacon mixture and the Parmesan cheese, and mix well.

» Season with salt and pepper to taste.

» Serve immediately, sprinkled with parsley if desired.

Mac & Cheese Burger Pie

Here's a favorite with the kids. It's important to use really lean ground beef in this recipe.

Serves 4 to 6

3/4 lb. hamburger - 90% lean or better
1/4 c. breadcrumbs
1/2 tbsp. minced onions
2 tbsp. ketchup
1/2 tbsp. prepared yellow mustard
1/4 tsp. salt
1 box macaroni & cheese
1/4 c. margarine
1/4 c. milk
1/2 cup shredded Cheddar cheese

» Preheat oven to 400 degrees.

» Mix the hamburger, breadcrumbs, onion, ketchup, mustard, and salt in a bowl.

» Shape the mixture into a 9-inch pie pan, patting evenly across the bottom and up the sides.

» Bake hamburger pie shell for 15 minutes.

» While hamburger is baking, prepare macaroni & cheese with milk and margarine according to directions on the box, or use your favorite variation.

» Remove the hamburger from oven and drain any excess grease.

» Scoop the mac & cheese into the burger pie shell.

» Sprinkle the shredded cheese over the top.

» Bake for another 10-15 minutes, or until the hamburger is completely cooked.

Cheesy Pasta

This is very cheesy, with a bold tomato flavor. There's nothing shy about this dish!

Serves 4

1 1/2 c. Favorite Tomato Sauce (below)
12 oz. fettuccine
3 tbsp. extra virgin olive oil
8 oz. Fontina cheese, shredded
1/2 c. grated Parmesan cheese
Black pepper
2 tbsp. chopped parsley

» Prepare tomato sauce according to directions below.

» While sauce is simmering, cook the fettuccine in boiling, salted water until al dente, then drain.

» Place the empty pot on the burner on Low, then pour in the olive oil, and tilt to cover the bottom of the pot.

» Return the fettuccine to the pot and stir until evenly coated with olive oil.

» Add the Fontina, and stir vigorously until it is melted and evenly distributed throughout the pasta. Turn up the heat a notch if necessary.

» Add the Parmesan, and stir into pasta, mixing thoroughly.

» Place a serving of fettuccine on one side of a plate, and sprinkle with freshly ground pepper and parsley. Spoon sauce onto other side of plate beside pasta.

Variations

» To save time, you could use a store-bought pasta sauce instead of making your own.

Favorite Tomato Sauce

Our favorite tomato sauce - yummy on any kind of pasta!

Makes 1 1/2 cups

3 tbsp. extra virgin olive oil
1/2 yellow onion, finely diced
1/4 c. dry red wine
14 oz. can tomato puree
1 tsp. salt
1 1/2 tsp. sugar
1/2 tsp. pepper
1 tsp. dried oregano

» Heat 2 tbsp. olive oil in a non-stick skillet over Medium-high heat, until hot but not smoking.

» Sauté onion in the skillet until translucent.

» Add wine to skillet. Cook until the wine is much reduced and you have a kind of purple onion slurry.

» Add the tomato puree, salt, sugar, pepper, and oregano.

» Simmer sauce 15-30 minutes, until thickened nicely.

» Just before serving stir remaining tbsp. olive oil into sauce.

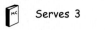

Cream of Mushroom Mac & Cheese

Just as fast as basic boxed mac & cheese, this version has a creamy mushroom flavor.

Serves 3

1 box macaroni & cheese
1/2 c. condensed cream of mushroom soup
1/4 c. margarine
3 tbsp. milk
Salt and pepper

» Cook the macaroni in boiling, salted water until it reaches desired doneness.

» Drain macaroni, and then return to pot.

» Add cream of mushroom soup and margarine to macaroni, and stir.

» Stir milk and cheese sauce from package into macaroni, and combine thoroughly.

» Season with salt and pepper to taste.

Variations

You can use different soups in this. Try cream of chicken, cream of celery, or cream of tomato.

ON THE STREET INTERVIEWS PRESENTS: Mac & Cheese

I like to look at my reflection in the spoon after I take a bite.

I like a guy who makes me Mac & Cheese on a date. Then I serve him dessert.

I like to eat my noodles one at a time until my Dad gets mad

Creole-Style Mac & Cheese

A dish for spicy food lovers! If you want to tone it down, you can substitute mild sausage for the hot links, and cut down on the Creole seasoning.

Serves 4

1 box macaroni & cheese
1/4 c. milk
1/4 c. margarine
2 tbsp. butter
1 c. onion, diced
2 cloves garlic, minced or pressed
2/3 c. celery, chopped
2/3 c. seeded and diced green bell pepper
1 tbsp. chopped parsley
1 tsp. Creole seasoning
1/2 lb. Louisiana hot links
Salt and pepper

» Prepare macaroni & cheese with milk and margarine according to directions on the box, or use your favorite variation.

» While macaroni is cooking, melt butter in a skillet over Medium heat.

» Sauté onion, garlic, celery, bell pepper, and parsley, until onion is translucent.

» Stir Creole seasoning into vegetables, mixing well.

» While vegetables are cooking, slice the hot links into 1/2-inch slices. Sauté them in a separate skillet until lightly browned.

» When macaroni & cheese is prepared, mix it together with vegetables and hot links.

» Season with salt and pepper to taste.

Variations

» Just omit the hot links for a great side dish.

French Onion Mac & Cheese

1 hour

Like French onion soup? This dish has the same rich flavors, without the soup! Four onions look like a lot, but they shrink tremendously as they're caramelized.

Serves 4

1/2 c. butter
4 medium onions, halved lengthwise and sliced thin
1/4 tsp. sugar
Salt and pepper
8 oz. dried elbow macaroni, or small shells
2 tbsp. olive oil
10 oz. Swiss or Gruyère cheese, shredded

» In a large skillet, melt butter over Medium heat.
» Add onions to skillet. Cover and cook 10 minutes, stirring occasionally.
» Remove the lid, and reduce heat to Medium-low. Sprinkle onions with sugar, and salt and pepper to taste.
» Cook uncovered, stirring frequently, 30-45 minutes, or until onions are a deep gold color. Onions should have a sweet flavor, and not be burned.
» When onions are close to done, cook macaroni in boiling, salted water, until al dente.
» Drain macaroni, then return to the pot, and toss with olive oil.
» Stir cheese into macaroni, until mixed thoroughly and melted.
» Season macaroni with salt and pepper to taste.
» Serve macaroni topped with onions.

Green Chili and Chicken Mac & Cheese

Green chilies add a bit of a kick to this Mexican-inspired version.

30 minutes

Serves 4

1 box macaroni & cheese
1/4 c. milk
1/4 c. margarine
1 tbsp. vegetable oil
1/4 c. onion, diced
1 1/2 c. cooked chicken, diced
6 oz. stewed tomatoes, drained and chopped
1 can (4.5 oz.) diced green chilies
1/4 c. sour cream
Salt and pepper
1/4 c. shredded Jack cheese
2 tbsp. chopped fresh cilantro

» Prepare macaroni & cheese with milk and margarine according to directions on the box, or use your favorite variation.

» While macaroni is cooking, heat oil in a large skillet, and sauté onion until translucent.

» Add chicken, tomatoes, and chilies to skillet, and stir well.

» Cover skillet, and cook over Low heat 10 minutes, stirring occasionally.

» Stir sour cream into skillet.

» Combine chicken mixture with macaroni & cheese, stirring to mix thoroughly.

» Season with salt and pepper to taste.

» Serve macaroni sprinkled with shredded cheese and cilantro.

Grilled Mac & Cheese Sandwich

30 minutes

Do you know somebody who adores grilled cheese sandwiches? Somebody who's also a nut for macaroni & cheese? The two favorites are combined in this surprising (and surprisingly yummy) dish.

This guy must really want us out of here.

Serves 4

1 box macaroni & cheese
1/4 c. milk
1/4 c. margarine + additional for bread
8 slices bacon (optional)
8 slices bread (white or whole wheat)
1 c. shredded Cheddar cheese
Chips (optional)
Pickles (optional)

» Prepare the macaroni & cheese according to box directions.

» While macaroni is cooking, cook bacon in a separate pan to the level of crispness you like. Drain bacon on paper towels.

» Spread margarine on one side of each piece of bread.

» Assemble sandwiches: Turn the first piece of bread so the margarine side is facing down. Top with a generous layer of mac & cheese. Add 2 slices bacon. Sprinkle with 1/4 c. Cheddar. Put second piece of bread on top, margarine side out. Repeat for 3 more sandwiches.

» Cook sandwiches over Medium heat, in a fry pan or on a griddle. When the first side is nicely browned, flip and cook the second side. Be careful when moving and flipping so the mac & cheese stays together.

» Serve with chips and pickles.

Variations

» **Garlic** – Skip the bacon. Sprinkle garlic salt lightly on each side of the sandwiches as they're cooking.

» **Open Face** – Eliminate top slice of bread. Cook sandwich in oven or microwave until cheese on top is melted. You could add a tomato slice to each sandwich, or sautéed mushrooms.

» **Mustard** – Spread your favorite mustard on the bread (opposite side from margarine) before assembling sandwich.

» **Different Cheese** – Try American cheese, Jack, or Mozzarella instead of Cheddar.

Mac & Cheese Low Fat Special

Why give up the food you love? This version is low fat, and has veggies to boot. You can eat this, and still feel good about your diet!

» Preheat oven to 350 degrees.

» Cook the macaroni until al dente, and drain.

» Return macaroni to pan. Add cheese sauce from package and milk, and stir until well combined. Do not add butter or margarine.

» While macaroni is cooking, spray a non-stick skillet with cooking spray.

» Sauté mushrooms in skillet over Medium heat, until lightly browned.

» Add spinach and red bell pepper to skillet. Cover skillet, and leave on heat for 2 minutes. Spinach should be wilted. Remove from heat.

» Stir veggies into macaroni & cheese. Season with salt and pepper to taste.

» Put macaroni and vegetable mixture into a shallow baking pan, patting down evenly. Bake for 30 minutes, or until top is barely beginning to brown.

Variations

» **Different Veggies** – Substitute your favorite vegetables, or whatever you have on hand. Broccoli, green beans, or tomatoes are all good options.

» **Chicken** – Add cooked chicken breast or white turkey meat.

Serves 3

1 box macaroni & cheese
1/4 cup fat free milk
1/4 lb. mushrooms, sliced
2 cups fresh spinach, coarsely chopped
1/2 red bell pepper, seeded and chopped
Salt and pepper

ON THE STREET INTERVIEWS PRESENTS: Mac & Cheese

The clumps of cheese and noodles remind me of me and my friends

I like to stuff noodles in my cheeks and pretend I'm a squirrel

My science prof says he thinks I might be related to the noodles!

Mac & Cheese Fiesta

Mexican flavors liven up this colorful supper dish.

45 minutes

Serves 4 to 6

1 box macaroni & cheese
1/4 c. milk
1/4 c. margarine
1 lb. ground beef
1 pkg. taco seasoning mix
1 large Roma tomato, sliced crosswise
1 c. shredded Jack cheese
2 tbsp. sliced black olives
1/2 avocado
1/2 tsp. lemon juice
2 tbsp. chopped fresh cilantro
Salsa (optional)
Sour cream (optional)

» Preheat oven to 375 degrees.

» Prepare macaroni & cheese with milk and margarine according to directions on the box, or use your favorite variation.

» While macaroni is cooking, cook ground beef in a large skillet over Medium heat, crumbling it apart as it cooks.

» Cook beef, stirring occasionally, until well browned.

» Drain off excess grease.

» Mix taco seasonings with beef according to package directions.

» Place macaroni & cheese in bottom of a baking dish. Top with ground beef mixture.

» Arrange tomatoes on top of beef, and then spread shredded cheese evenly on top, followed by olives.

» Bake for 25 minutes, or until cheese is bubbly.

» While dish is baking, peel, pit, and slice avocado.

» Toss slices with lemon juice so they don't turn brown.

» Remove dish from oven when ready. Arrange avocados slices between tomatoes, and sprinkle top of dish with chopped cilantro.

» Serve garnished with salsa and/ or sour cream.

Meatballs - Mexican

These meatballs have Mexican spices, and are simmered in a tomato-based sauce.

1 hour

Serves 4

1 pkg. taco seasoning

1/4 c. fine fresh breadcrumbs

1 egg, beaten lightly

1 lb. ground beef, or combined ground beef and pork

Salt and pepper

2 tbsp. olive oil

1/2 large onion, chopped

1/2 red bell pepper, seeded and chopped

1/2 green bell pepper, seeded and chopped

1 can (14-1/2 oz.) crushed tomatoes

Tabasco® sauce

1 box macaroni & cheese

1/4 c. milk

1/4 c. margarine

» Combine taco seasoning and breadcrumbs in a large bowl.

» Add ground meat and egg to bowl, and combine all ingredients well.

» Shape the meat into walnut-sized meatballs.

» Heat olive oil in a large skillet, and sauté the onion until softened.

» Add green and red bell peppers, and sauté until peppers are softened.

» Add tomatoes to skillet with 1/3 c. water, and stir to mix well.

» Add enough Tabasco® sauce to reach desired spiciness, and season with salt and pepper to taste.

» Add meatballs to sauce. Cover skillet and simmer 30 minutes, stirring occasionally.

» While meatballs are simmering, prepare macaroni & cheese with milk and margarine according to directions on the box, or use your favorite variation.

» Season macaroni with salt and pepper to taste.

» Serve macaroni & cheese with meatballs and sauce on top.

Meatballs - Swedish

These meatballs are baked, and then served with gravy.

Serves 4

1/3 c. milk

1/2 c. fine fresh breadcrumbs

1/3 c. finely chopped onion

1 lb. ground beef, or combined ground beef and pork

1 egg, beaten lightly

Salt and pepper

1 package brown gravy mix

1 box macaroni & cheese

1/4 c. milk

1/4 c. margarine

» Preheat oven to 400 degrees.

» Combine milk and breadcrumbs in a large bowl, then let stand 5 minutes.

» Add onion, meat, egg, and salt and pepper, and stir until combined well.

» Shape the meat into walnut-sized meatballs, and place on a lightly oiled cookie sheet, leaving space between them.

» Bake meatballs. Turn them after 10 minutes, and then every 5 minutes after that, so that they brown on all sides.

» Bake 25-30 minutes, or until well browned.

» While meatballs are baking, make gravy according to package directions.

» Prepare macaroni & cheese with milk and margarine according to directions on the box, or use your favorite variation.

» Serve macaroni & cheese with meatballs and gravy on top.

Mega Lasagna

1 hour + 30 minutes

Here's a mega cheesy dish that will appeal to guys with big appetites. It's super-rich, filling, and delicious.

Serves 6

1 pkg. (16 oz.) lasagna noodles
1/4 lb. Cheddar cheese
1/4 lb. Fontina cheese
1/4 lb. Jack cheese
1/4 lb. Mozzarella
1 tbsp. + 2 tsp. extra virgin olive oil
3 c. Favorite Tomato Sauce (p. 46)

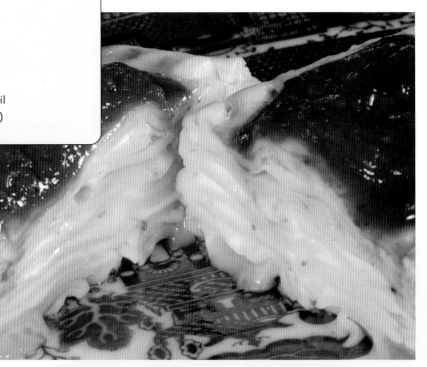

» Preheat oven to 425 degrees.

» Cook the lasagna noodles in salted water, according to package directions. Don't boil too hard, and stir to keep them from sticking together.

» While noodles are cooking, grate all cheeses, and mix them together.

» When the noodles are al dente, place the pot under cold, running water. Keep stirring and draining to rinse the pasta well. When the water stays fairly clear, drain the noodles in a colander.

» Return noodles to pot. Pour 1 tbsp. olive oil over the noodles and stir to coat them.

» Grease the inside of a deep 4 x 9-inch glass baking dish with 1 tsp. olive oil.

» Place a layer of noodles in the bottom of the pan.

Cut them to fit so they lay fairly flat without much overlap. You might want to create a noodle as the standard size to cut to.

» Sprinkle 1/2 c. cheese evenly over the noodles.

» Continue layering the noodles and cheese until you have 7 layers of noodles, ending with noodles on top. You should have enough noodles left over for one extra layer.

» Coat the top layer with 1 tsp. olive oil.

» Place 1 layer of "sacrificial" noodles on top, to protect the top layer while cooking. Press the lasagna gently but firmly into the pan.

» Bake the lasagna for 30 minutes, until you see all layers bubbling while cooking.

» Remove from oven, and let cool at room temperature for 30 minutes. Discard "sacrificial" noodle layer.

» Remove the lasagna from the dish by running a knife around the inside of the edges, and then turning it upside down onto a large dish or cutting board. Knock on the top of the pan to remove it.

» Place lasagna on serving dish, and pour sauce over it. Cut in slices, and serve with extra sauce on the side.

Variations

» **Different Cheese** –
You could change the proportions of
the cheese mix, or swap one of them
for another cheese like Havarti.

» **Different Sauce** –
Instead of making the Favorite
Tomato Sauce, you can substitute
your own favorite homemade or
store-bought pasta sauce.

Mac & Cheese
COLOGNE FOR MEN

Mac & Cheese Paella

This dish has a variety of flavors, lots of protein, and just a bit of a bite to it.

1 hour

Serves 4

4 chicken thighs, skin removed
Salt and pepper
1 pinch + 1 tsp. paprika
2 tbsp. olive oil
1/2 lb. linguica sausage, sliced diagonally 1/4-inch thick
1/2 small onion, diced
3 cloves garlic, minced or pressed
1/2 red bell pepper, seeded and diced
1/2 medium tomato, chopped
1/2 c. chopped fresh parsley
Dash of Tabasco® sauce
1 c. chicken stock
1/4 c. dry white wine
Pinch of saffron
1/4 lb. medium shrimp, peeled, tail left on if desired
1 box macaroni & cheese
1/4 c. milk
1/4 c. margarine

» Preheat oven to 350 degrees.
» Season chicken thighs with salt and pepper, and rub with a pinch of paprika.
» Heat olive oil in a large skillet over Medium-high heat until hot but not smoking.
» Brown chicken and sausage in skillet until browned on all sides, about 5-10 minutes, then remove to a plate.
» Add onion, garlic, and bell pepper to the skillet. Cook, stirring occasionally, until onion is softened.
» Add tomato, parsley and Tabasco® sauce to skillet, and cook 3 minutes.
» Add chicken stock, white wine, saffron, and remaining 1 tsp. paprika to skillet. Boil 5 minutes.
» Season sauce with salt and pepper to taste.
» Stir chicken, sausage, and shrimp into skillet.
» Put skillet in oven and bake, uncovered, 10 minutes.
» Stir well, then bake 20 minutes more.
» Prepare macaroni & cheese with milk and margarine according to directions on the box, or use your favorite variation.
» Serve macaroni & cheese topped with paella.

Variations

» For a spicier version, you can use spicy sausage or more Tabasco® sauce.

Pepper Steak Mac & Cheese

Meat, vegetables, pasta, and dairy products - this recipe has them all.

1 hour

Serves 3

3/4 lb. boneless beef
1 tbsp. olive oil
Salt and pepper
1/4 c. chopped onion
1 large clove garlic, minced or pressed
1 c. beef broth
1 box macaroni & cheese
1/4 c. milk
1/4 c. margarine
1/2 red bell pepper, seeded and cut into strips
3/4 c. frozen green beans
1 c. canned sliced stewed tomatoes, drained
3 tbsp. cornstarch

» Cut beef in strips 1/4-inch thick, 1/2-inch wide and 2-inches long, removing as much fat as possible.

» Heat oil in a large skillet, and brown beef over Medium-high heat. Season beef with salt and pepper while it's cooking.

» When beef is browned, remove it with a slotted spoon to a bowl.

» Lower heat to Medium. Add onion and garlic to skillet, and sauté until onion is translucent. Add more oil if necessary.

» Return beef to skillet, and add beef broth.

» Cover skillet, and simmer for 25 to 30 minutes, until beef is tender.

» While beef is simmering, prepare macaroni & cheese with milk and margarine according to directions on the box, or use your favorite variation.

» Add pepper, beans, and tomatoes to skillet. Cover, and simmer 10 minutes.

» Mix corn starch with 1/4 c. cold water, then stir into skillet mixture.

» Cook uncovered, stirring frequently, 5 minutes or until thickened.

» Season beef mixture with salt and pepper to taste.

» Serve macaroni & cheese topped with beef.

Macaroni & Cheese Pizza

What's the dullest thing about pizza? The crust! So why not replace that bland doughy stuff with noodles and cheese? This recipe makes a deep-dish pizza that you eat with a fork. Just add your favorite toppings and enjoy!

1 hour

Serves 4 to 6

12 oz. egg noodles

5 tbsp. olive oil

1 lb. Fontina cheese, shredded

1/2 onion, chopped

1/4 c. red wine

14 oz. can tomato puree

1/2 tbsp. oregano

1/2 tbsp. sugar

Salt and pepper

1/2 lb. Italian sausage

2 oz. sliced pepperoni

1/2 green bell pepper, seeded & diced

1/2 c. grated Parmesan cheese

Make the "crust"

» Preheat oven to 450 degrees.

» Bring a large pot of water to a boil. Cook noodles until al dente, and then 1 minute longer.

» Drain noodles.

» Pour 2 tbsp. olive oil into the empty pot. Return noodles to the pot, and toss well with oil.

» Stir 12 oz. of grated Fontina into noodles, and mix well.

» Spray a 12-inch ovenproof skillet or baking pan with non-stick spray. Spread noodle mixture into pan, pressing evenly across the bottom and up the sides.

» Bake 13-17 minutes, until crust seems fairly firm.

» Remove from oven and keep warm.

While "crust" is baking, prepare sauce & toppings

» Sauté onion in 1 tbsp. olive oil until soft and golden.

» Add wine to onions, and boil until reduced by half.

*"This was more than terrific!!
My kids simply adored the idea
and the taste."*

*- Ruby P. Sanjana,
Mumbai, India*

» Add to sauce: tomato puree, oregano, sugar, 2 tbsp. olive oil, salt and pepper to taste. Simmer sauce 15 minutes more, or until thickened.

» In a separate skillet, brown sausage, stirring and breaking apart.

» When sausage is well browned, add pepperoni slices and cook until lightly browned. Remove from heat.

Make pizza

» Spoon sauce on top of noodle crust, spreading evenly.

» Spread remaining 4 oz. Fontina over pizza.

» Top with sausage, pepperoni, and bell pepper, then sprinkle with Parmesan.

» Bake pizza 5-10 minutes, until bubbling.

Variations

» **Thin crust** – For a thin crust you can pick up with your hands, use 8 oz. angel hair pasta. Cook according to package directions. Use just 8 oz. Fontina in the crust, add 2 beaten eggs to the crust ingredients, and bake it on a shallow pizza pan instead of in a deep skillet.

» **Different toppings** – Use whatever toppings you like ... the possibilities are endless!

» **Faster & easier version** – Use store-bought pasta sauce instead of making the sauce, and your pizza will be oven ready in no time.

Mac & Cheese Trivia

In 1993, Crayola crayons added a color named "macaroni and cheese".

The military's Meals, Ready to Eat have a 3-year shelf life, can be dropped from helicopters without parachutes, and contain their own chemical heating device for hot meals anywhere. Unfortunately, current MRE technology turns macaroni soggy and cheese green. But they're working on it!

In the south, macaroni & cheese is often considered a vegetable, and is listed that way in the index of some cookbooks.

In times of stress, many people long for foods they ate in their less stressful younger days. What you eat as a child becomes comfort food – macaroni & cheese!

Postulated: WE ARE WHAT WE EAT
Therefore, EINSTEIN = MACARONI and CHEESE

$$E=MC^2$$ Lotsa

E = MAC & CHEESE

E = M____SE²

CH_____CARONI

In the 1880's, 1200 Italian laborers began constructing a railway line through Victoria, TX. Their staple food was shipped from Italy in large wooden boxes stamped MACARONI. That's how the New York, Texas and Mexican Railway became known as the Macaroni Line.

One method recommended to avoid post-St. Patrick's Day hangovers: eat a large macaroni & cheese dinner before beginning the celebrations.

Mac & Cheese Primavera

Need to eat more veggies? Check out this tasty and colorful dish.

Serves 3

1 box macaroni & cheese
1/4 c. milk
1/4 c. margarine
1 tbsp. olive oil
1 tbsp. butter
1 clove garlic, minced or pressed
1/2 c. red bell pepper, seeded and diced
1/2 c. zucchini, halved lengthwise and sliced
1/2 c. broccoli florets
1/2 c. cauliflower florets
1/4 c. grated Parmesan cheese plus extra to top
Salt and pepper
2 tbsp. finely chopped fresh parsley

» Prepare macaroni & cheese with milk and margarine according to directions on the box, or use your favorite variation.
» While macaroni is cooking, heat oil and butter in a large skillet over Medium heat.
» Add garlic to skillet, and cook 1 minute.
» Add all vegetables to skillet. Season vegetables with salt and pepper.
» Cook vegetables, stirring occasionally, for 6 minutes, or until tender.
» After macaroni & cheese is prepared, stir in the vegetables, and 1/4 c. Parmesan cheese.
» Add salt and pepper to taste.
» Serve macaroni & cheese topped with parsley and additional Parmesan as desired.

Variations

You can use different combinations of vegetables. Almost anything goes, just use a total of 2 cups of vegetables. The following all work well: Tomatoes, Green beans, Yellow crookneck squash, Green bell pepper, Snow peas.

Mac & Cheese with Prosciutto and Peas

This dish is quick to prepare, but adds a touch of class to your mac & cheese.

Serves 3

1 box macaroni & cheese
1/4 c. milk
1/4 c. margarine
1/3 c. frozen peas
2 tbsp. butter or margarine
2 tbsp. dry white wine
1/3 c. half & half
2 oz. prosciutto, cut in matchstick slices
Salt and pepper
1/4 c. grated Parmesan cheese

» Prepare macaroni & cheese with milk and margarine according to directions on the box, or use your favorite variation.

» While the macaroni is cooking, sauté the peas in a small skillet with butter or margarine and white wine for 2-3 minutes.

» Add half & half and prosciutto to skillet, and simmer 3 minutes.

» When macaroni is prepared, stir peas and prosciutto mixture into macaroni.

» Season with salt and pepper to taste.

» Serve macaroni and sprinkle with Parmesan.

Jazz greats -
Lenny Prosciutto &
Blind Man Peas

30 minutes

Mac & Cheese with Sausage, Red Peppers and Corn

This recipe is great for a busy night, with its wonderful, warming flavors.

Serves 3 to 4

1 box macaroni & cheese
1/4 c. milk
1/4 c. margarine
1/2 lb. mild Italian sausage
1 small jar roasted red peppers, drained and chopped
1 small can of sweet corn kernels, drained
Salt and pepper

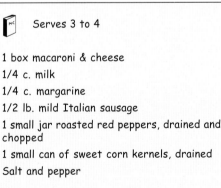

"Wonderful, and I shall be sure to try it again."
- Shirley W., Nova Scotia, Canada

» Prepare macaroni & cheese with milk and margarine according to directions on the box, or use your favorite variation.
» While macaroni is cooking, remove the Italian sausage from its casings, if necessary.
» In a large skillet over Medium heat, brown the sausage well, breaking it into small pieces.
» When the sausage is browned, drain on paper towels.
» After the mac & cheese is prepared, mix in the sausage, peppers, and corn.
» Season with salt and pepper to taste, and serve.

Variations
Spicy – Try spicy Italian sausage, if you're looking for a bolder taste.

Mac & Cheese Shepherd's Pie

This takes a while to bake, but there's not too much active working time. It's wonderful when it's cold outside!

× 1 hour 15 minutes

📕 Serves 4

1 box macaroni & cheese
1/4 c. milk
1/4 c. margarine
1 lb. ground beef
1 tbsp. olive oil
1/2 medium onion, diced
1/2 c. carrot, diced small
1 large clove garlic, minced or pressed
4 oz. mushrooms, sliced (optional)
1/2 c. dry red wine
3/4 c. canned tomato sauce
1/2 tsp. dried thyme
Salt and pepper
1/2 c. shredded Jack cheese

» Preheat oven to 350 degrees.

» Prepare macaroni & cheese with milk and margarine according to directions on the box, or use your favorite variation.

» While macaroni is cooking, brown ground beef in a large skillet over Medium heat, breaking into small chunks as it cooks.

» When beef is browned, remove it to a bowl, draining excess grease.

» Return skillet to heat, and add olive oil. Heat until hot but not smoking, over Medium-high heat.

» Sauté onion, carrot, and garlic for 5 minutes, stirring occasionally.

» Add optional mushrooms to skillet. Cook, stirring occasionally, until mushrooms are browned.

» Add red wine to pan, and boil until reduced by half.

» Add beef to pan, along with tomato sauce, thyme, and salt and pepper to taste.

» Simmer mixture 5 minutes, and then pour into a deep pie dish.

» Spoon macaroni & cheese over beef mixture, creating an even layer on top.

» Sprinkle shredded cheese over top of pie.

» Bake pie for 45 minutes, or until top is bubbling and starting to brown.

Variations

» **Quick & Easy** – For the beef mixture, just brown 1 lb. ground beef. Prepare 1 package of brown gravy mix according to package directions, and stir into beef. Top with macaroni & cheese, and bake as above.

Sloppy Corn Checkerboard

This dish looks harder than it is, but the components are each quite easy to make.

45 minutes

Serves 4 to 6

1 box macaroni & cheese
1/4 c. milk
1/4 c. margarine
2 1/2 c. shredded Jack cheese
1 lb. ground beef
1 can Sloppy Joe seasoning
3 c. frozen white corn

Prepare components

» Prepare macaroni & cheese with milk and margarine according to directions on the box, or use your favorite variation.

» Stir 1/2 c. Jack cheese into macaroni, reserving the other 2 c. for the corn.

» While macaroni is cooking, brown ground beef, breaking it apart into small pieces as it cooks.

» When beef is well browned, drain off excess grease.

» Mix Sloppy Joe seasoning into ground beef.

» While beef is cooking, heat the corn in a small pot over low heat.

» When corn is hot, add the reserved 2 c. Jack cheese. Stir until cheese is fully melted and evenly distributed.

Assemble and Bake

» This recipe could use two 13-inch x 9-inch baking dishes, or just one, depending on how you scoop the ingredients.

» For optimal preparation, use a separate serving spoon for each of the three components.

» Place a large spoonful of each component into the baking dish, one after the other in a row. See picture for finished pattern.

» For the checkerboard pattern, place one row at a time, always alternating the components in the same order: Sloppy Joe, mac & cheese, corn, etc.

» Start each row with the next component in sequence. If one row started with Sloppy Joe, the next row should start with mac & cheese, etc. Keep following the same pattern until the dish is filled.

» Bake 10 to 15 minutes, or until the cheese in the corn starts to bubble.

Mac & Cheese Sloppy Joes

Here's one the kids will love!

Serves 4

1 box macaroni & cheese
1/4 c. milk
1/4 c. margarine
1 lb. ground beef
1 packet or can of your favorite Sloppy Joe mix
4 slices of American cheese (optional)
4 large hamburger buns

» Prepare macaroni & cheese with milk and margarine according to directions on the box, or use your favorite variation.
» While macaroni is cooking, brown the ground beef in a large skillet, breaking apart as it cooks.
» When beef is well browned, drain excess grease.
» Prepare Sloppy Joe mix according to package directions, and stir into ground beef.
» Place cheese slice (if desired) on the bottom of a bun, cover with mac & cheese, and top with the Sloppy Joe mixture.

Mac & Cheese in the Movies

Can you spot the macaroni and cheese in these movies?

» "While You Were Sleeping" (Sandra Bullock)
» "The Truman Show" (Jim Carrey)
» "Soul Food" (Vanessa Williams)
» "Metro" (Eddie Murphy)
» "One Special Night" (James Garner and Julie Andrews)
» "What's Cooking?" (Julianna Marguiles)
» "Ballistic: Ecks vs. Severs" (Lucy Liu)

Southwest Mac & Cheese

Southwestern flavors add zing to mac & cheese in this dish.

Serves 3

1 box macaroni & cheese
1/4 c. milk
1/4 c. margarine
1 can (14.5 oz.) Mexican-style stewed tomatoes
3 tbsp. diced canned green chilies
1 small can (7 oz.) corn
1 tsp. seeded and minced fresh jalapeño pepper
3 tbsp. chopped fresh cilantro

» Prepare macaroni & cheese with milk and margarine according to directions on the box, or use your favorite variation.

» While macaroni is cooking, drain and dice tomatoes and green chilies.

» When macaroni is prepared, stir in tomatoes, chilies, corn, and jalapeño.

» Cook macaroni & cheese over Low heat, stirring occasionally, until all ingredients are heated through.

» Serve mac & cheese sprinkled with cilantro.

Mac & Cheese Stuffed Bell Peppers

These stuffed peppers make a light main course. Serve with a salad, or extra filling.

1 hour

Serves 4

1 box macaroni & cheese
1/4 c. milk
1/4 c. margarine
2 tbsp. olive oil
2 shallots, minced
2 cloves garlic, minced or pressed
3/4 lb. mild Italian sausage, removed from casings
1/4 c. minced fresh parsley
1 tsp. dried thyme
Salt and pepper
4 green or red bell peppers
2 tbsp. grated Parmesan cheese

» Preheat oven to 350 degrees.
» Prepare macaroni & cheese with milk and margarine according to directions on the box, or use your favorite variation.
» While macaroni is cooking, sauté shallots and garlic in a large skillet, until softened.
» Add sausage to skillet. Cook, breaking into small pieces, until well browned.
» Drain sausage mixture on paper towels.
» When mac & cheese is prepared, stir in sausage mixture, parsley, and thyme, mixing thoroughly.
» Season with salt and pepper to taste.
» Cut off stem ends of bell peppers. Remove ribs and seeds, leaving peppers intact.
» Fill peppers with macaroni & cheese, pressing down firmly.
» Sprinkle Parmesan over top of peppers.
» Arrange peppers in a baking dish, ensuring they stand up straight. Put stem ends back on top.
» Pour 1 c. water into baking dish, and bake 45 minutes. Peppers should be soft when done.

Mac & Cheese in Politics

Macaroni and cheese was one of former president Ronald Reagan's favorite meals. He ate it aboard Air Force One, and while in the hospital recovering from gunshot wounds. He also had it at his 84th birthday party, where he thanked everyone for the well-wishes "on the 45th anniversary of my 39th birthday".

At the 1996 GOP Convention, the San Diego Host Committee handed out "goody bags" to the delegates. Among other things, these included boxes of macaroni & cheese with pasta shaped like elephants, and (appropriately enough) Dole brand raisins.

The Congressional lunch for Bill Clinton after his 1997 swearing in ceremony included macaroni & cheese, in timbales made with sheep's milk cheese. The recipe was based on a historical cookbook by Mary Randolph – a cousin of Thomas Jefferson, another macaroni & cheese lover.

At a women's rally during the 2000 Gore-Lieberman campaign, women in the crowd were given boxes of macaroni & cheese to shake like noisemakers as they cheered.

CAN'T WE ALL JUST GET ALONG?
(a Public Service Message from Mac & Cheese)

Mac & Cheese with Tomatoes, Olives and Goat Cheese

Goat cheese with your macaroni? It makes all the difference in this quick and easy recipe filled with bold Mediterranean flavors.

Serves 3

2 Roma tomatoes, seeded and chopped
3 tbsp. drained and chopped sun-dried tomatoes in oil
1/4 c. Kalamata olives, pitted and chopped
1 clove garlic, minced
1 tbsp. extra virgin olive oil
1/2 tbsp. balsamic vinegar
1/2 tsp. dried thyme
1 box macaroni & cheese
1/4 c. milk
1/4 c. margarine
3 oz. mild goat cheese + additional for top
Salt and pepper
1 tbsp. chopped fresh parsley

» Combine fresh and dried tomatoes, olives, garlic, olive oil, vinegar, and thyme in a glass bowl. Stir to mix well, then let stand at room temperature.

» Prepare macaroni & cheese with milk and margarine according to directions on the box, or use your favorite variation. After mac & cheese is prepared, place it back in pot.

» Add 3 oz. goat cheese to macaroni. Cook briefly over Low heat, stirring, until cheese is melted and mixture is smooth.

» Season macaroni with salt and pepper to taste.

» Put macaroni & cheese on plates. Spoon tomato-olive mixture over macaroni, and sprinkle remaining goat cheese and parsley on top.

Tuna Casserole

Here's a mac & cheese take on the old classic.

Serves 4

1 box macaroni & cheese
1/4 c. milk
3/4 c. condensed cream of mushroom soup
1 can (6 oz.) tuna fish packed in water, drained
1/2 tsp. dried dill weed + 1 pinch for top
Salt and pepper
1/4 c. shredded Jack cheese
1/4 c. shredded Cheddar cheese

» Preheat oven to 375 degrees.
» Cook the macaroni in boiling, salted water until al dente. Drain and return to empty pot.
» Add milk, condensed soup, and contents of cheese packet to macaroni, and stir until combined well.
» Stir in tuna fish and 1/2 tsp. dill weed, mixing thoroughly.
» Season with salt and pepper.
» Put macaroni into a baking dish, smoothing the top.
» Spread shredded Jack and Cheddar cheeses on top of casserole.
» Sprinkle a pinch of dill weed on top of cheese.
» Bake 20 minutes, until just starting to brown.

Turkey Macaroni Casserole

1 hour

Here's a delicious use for leftover turkey. The cranberries brighten the dish with bursts of flavor. Serve with a green salad for a simple dinner.

Serves 4

1 box macaroni & cheese
1/4 c. milk
1/4 c. margarine
2 tbsp. butter
1/4 onion, chopped
1 large clove garlic, minced or pressed
4 oz. mushrooms, sliced
Salt and pepper
1/2 c. dry white wine
1 c. frozen green beans
1 1/2 c. cooked turkey meat, cut into 1-inch pieces
1/4 tsp. dried thyme
2 tbsp. minced fresh parsley
2 eggs
3/4 c. milk
1/2 c. shredded Jack cheese
1/4 c. fresh cranberries

» Preheat oven to 375 degrees.
» Prepare macaroni & cheese with milk and margarine according to directions on the box, or use your favorite variation.
» While macaroni is cooking, heat butter in a large skillet over Medium-high heat.
» Add onion and garlic to skillet, and sauté until just soft.
» Add mushrooms to skillet, and sauté until they've given off their liquid.
» Season mushrooms lightly with salt and pepper as they cook.
» Add white wine to skillet, and boil 3 minutes, until much reduced but not completely evaporated.
» Add green beans to skillet, and cook just until thawed.
» In a large bowl, combine macaroni & cheese, mushroom mixture, turkey, thyme, and parsley. Mix well.
» Season with salt and pepper to taste.
» Pour macaroni mixture into a 2 qt. baking dish, spreading evenly.
» Beat eggs with milk in a large cup, and pour evenly over top of casserole.
» Spread shredded cheese on top of casserole.
» Sprinkle cranberries on top, pressing down lightly.
» Bake 30-40 minutes, until heated through and top begins to brown.

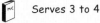

Wild Mushroom Mac & Cheese

This is a richly flavored mushroom dish, accented with garlic, sherry and thyme.

Serves 3 to 4

1 box macaroni & cheese

1/4 c. milk

1/4 c. margarine

1/2 lb. fresh button mushrooms, sliced

1/2 lb. mixed fresh wild mushrooms (such as shiitake, chanterelle, porcini, or portobello), sliced

1 c. finely chopped onion

2 tbsp. olive oil

2 cloves garlic, minced or pressed

Salt and pepper

1/2 c. dry sherry

1/4 tsp. dried thyme

Fresh parsley, minced, to sprinkle on top

Grated Parmesan to sprinkle on top

» Prepare macaroni & cheese with milk and margarine according to directions on the box, or use your favorite variation.

» If you're using large wild mushrooms, cut them into pieces about the same size as the sliced button mushrooms.

» In a large skillet, sauté the onion in olive oil, over Medium heat until softened.

» Add garlic to the skillet, and sauté 1 minute.

» Add mushrooms to skillet, and season with salt and pepper. Cook, stirring occasionally, until the mushrooms have given off their liquid (about 10-15 minutes).

» Add sherry and thyme to skillet. Simmer 5-10 minutes, until liquid is greatly reduced.

» Season mushrooms with salt and pepper to taste.

» Serve the macaroni topped with the mushrooms.

» Sprinkle parsley and Parmesan on top.

Mac & Cheese with Zucchini, Basil, and Parmesan

Even non-zucchini-fans have been known to say this dish is delicious!

Serves 3

1 box macaroni & cheese
1/4 c. milk
1/4 c. margarine
1 medium-large zucchini, halved lengthwise then sliced
1 tbsp. olive oil
3 tbsp. chopped fresh basil leaves + 6 whole basil leaves
Salt and pepper
1/2 c. grated Parmesan cheese

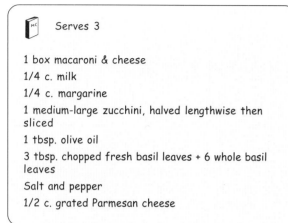

» Prepare macaroni & cheese with milk and margarine according to directions on the box, or use your favorite variation.

» While the macaroni is cooking, sauté the zucchini slices in olive oil over Medium-high heat, until starting to brown. Sprinkle zucchini with salt and pepper as it cooks.

» Reserve 6 nice basil leaves for garnish, and chop enough to give 3 tbsp. chopped basil.

» When mac & cheese is prepared, add zucchini, chopped basil, and 1/4 c. of the Parmesan, combining thoroughly.

» Season with salt and pepper to taste.

» Divide macaroni among serving dishes.

» Sprinkle remaining Parmesan over each dish, and garnish with reserved basil leaves.

Variations

» **Use different herbs** – fresh parsley, thyme or oregano would give this dish quite a different flavor.

» **Add 2 Roma tomatoes**, seeded and chopped.

» **Substitute** yellow squash or pattypan squash for zucchini.

Chapter 4

Mac & Cheese Bits & Bites:
APPETIZERS
Sides & Salads

Mac & Cheese Appetizers

*Hors d'oeuvres anyone? Here are three different quick and easy macaroni & cheese appetizers.
Each makes a nifty presentation without a lot of effort.*

× 1 hour
1 hour chill

1 box macaroni & cheese
1/4 c. milk
1/4 c. margarine

» Prepare macaroni & cheese with milk and margarine according to directions on the box, or use your favorite variation, and then follow the instructions for selected appetizers below.

» 1 box of mac & cheese can make all 3 of these appetizer recipes.

Deviled Eggs
Makes 12 appetizers

6 eggs
4 tsp. Dijon mustard
2 tbsp. mayonnaise
1 tbsp. finely chopped fresh cilantro
3/4 tsp. wine vinegar
1/4 tsp. Tabasco® sauce, or to taste
Paprika or chopped chives

» Hard boil eggs, and remove shells.
» Cut eggs in half lengthwise. Remove yolks carefully, preserving whites. Place yolks in a bowl.
» Crush egg yolks thoroughly with a fork.
» Add mustard, mayonnaise, cilantro, vinegar, and Tabasco® to bowl. Mix well.
» Add 3/4 c. mac & cheese to bowl and mix well.
» Spoon egg yolk mixture into the depressions in the egg whites, creating a small mound in each egg.
» Sprinkle paprika or chives over eggs.

Salami Macaroni Canapés

Makes about 24 appetizers

8 slices rye bread
Mustard (Dijon or your choice)
1/4 lb. sliced salami
2 1/4 oz. can sliced black olives

» Spread bread with mustard.
» Cover bread with 1 layer of salami slices, overlapping as needed.
» Cut bread and salami into canapé shapes with a cookie cutter, or cut into triangles with a knife, removing the crust.
» Place a small mound of mac & cheese in the center of each canapé, and top with a slice of olive.
» Serve cold.

Ham & Cheese Roll-ups

Makes about 30 appetizers

1/2 lb. sliced ham
Mustard (hot & sweet honey, or your choice)

» Spread slices of ham with mustard of your choice. We liked hot & sweet honey mustard.
» Cover ham slice with a thin, even layer of mac & cheese, leaving a 1-inch space uncovered at each end.
» Roll up ham slices, ending with an uncovered edge. Secure each roll-up with 5 evenly spaced toothpicks.
» Refrigerate roll-ups for at least 1 hour.
» Cut each ham roll-up into 5 pieces, so that each has a toothpick for serving.
» Keep refrigerated until serving.

SCIENCE NEWS

Eager scientists attempt to transplant the gene
of a noodle to a cow to create ready-to-eat Mac & Cheese.

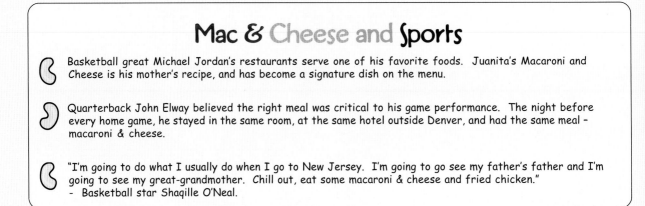

KAZAM!!

oops, wrong genes

Mac & Cheese and Sports

Basketball great Michael Jordan's restaurants serve one of his favorite foods. Juanita's Macaroni and Cheese is his mother's recipe, and has become a signature dish on the menu.

Quarterback John Elway believed the right meal was critical to his game performance. The night before every home game, he stayed in the same room, at the same hotel outside Denver, and had the same meal – macaroni & cheese.

"I'm going to do what I usually do when I go to New Jersey. I'm going to go see my father's father and I'm going to see my great-grandmother. Chill out, eat some macaroni & cheese and fried chicken."
- Basketball star Shaquille O'Neal.

Mac & Cheese Balls **with Marinara Sauce**

You've tried fried mozzarella sticks for dipping, now give these a try for a new, lighter twist!

× 1 hour 30 minutes

Makes about 20-30 mac & cheese balls

1 box macaroni & cheese
1/4 c. margarine
1/4 c. milk
1 cup shredded Cheddar cheese
1 egg
About 2 cups seasoned bread crumbs
Your favorite marinara sauce for dipping

» Make the macaroni and cheese with milk and margarine, according to box directions, or your favorite variation.

» Add the cheese and the egg and stir well.

» Place the prepared macaroni and cheese in a large bowl and place in refrigerator for half an hour or more, till it's chilled through.

» Preheat oven to 350 degrees.

» Place the bread crumbs in a bowl.

» Once the mac and cheese is chilled, use a spoon to scoop out the mac and cheese and then form it in your hands into a fairly compact ball (you may want to oil your hands first).

» Roll the ball in the breadcrumbs till lightly covered.

» Place the balls on a nonstick baking sheet.

» After you have made them all, cook in the oven for 15 minutes.

» After cooking, let cool to room temperature before eating, to ensure maximum hold.

Broccoli with Gorgonzola Shells

Here's an appetizer with bright color and full flavors.

 Serves 4

1 1/2 c. small shell pasta, dried
2 tbsp. olive oil
4 c. broccoli florets
Salt and pepper
1/4 c. milk
6 oz. Gorgonzola cheese, cut into bits
2 tbsp. pine nuts

» Cook pasta in boiling salted water until al dente. Drain, then return to pan.

» While pasta is cooking, put 1/2 c. water and olive oil in a large skillet, and bring to a boil over Medium-high heat.

» Add broccoli to skillet, cover, and cook 5 minutes.

» Uncover skillet. Cook until water is evaporated, and broccoli is tender and beginning to brown. Sprinkle lightly with salt.

» When done, remove broccoli from heat and keep warm.

» Add milk to pasta, and heat over Low heat until hot, stirring frequently.

» Stir Gorgonzola into pasta and cook, stirring, until cheese is melted.

» Season pasta with salt and pepper to taste.

» Serve pasta topped with broccoli, and sprinkle with pine nuts.

ON THE STREET INTERVIEWS PRESENTS: Mac & Cheese

I like to shake the box and samba.

My dog likes it when I put the empty cheese packet on her nose

I used to wear a noodle in my right ear.

Mac & Cheese Cobb Salad

Here's a twist on the standard Cobb Salad - why not make it with macaroni & cheese?

30 minute + 1 hour chill

Serves 2 as a main course

1 box macaroni & cheese
1/4 c. milk
3 tbsp. margarine
2 tbsp. blue cheese salad dressing
Salt and pepper
3 strips bacon
1 avocado, peeled, pitted and chopped
1 tsp. lemon juice
2 Roma tomatoes, chopped
1 tbsp. chopped fresh chives

» Make the macaroni & cheese with milk and margarine according to box directions, but use only 3 tbsp. margarine.

» Mix blue cheese salad dressing into macaroni & cheese.

» Season macaroni with salt and pepper to taste, and then chill until cool.

» Cook bacon until crisp. Drain on paper towels, then crumble.

» Pit, peel and chop avocado, and toss with lemon juice.

» Divide macaroni between 2 large plates.

» Arrange tomato, avocado, and bacon on top of macaroni.

» Sprinkle chives over top of salads, and serve.

Variations

» Add chicken or turkey - Add chunks of pre-cooked white chicken or turkey meat to salad.

Corn Macaroni Custards with Roasted Red Pepper Sauce

1 hour

The rich corn, hint of cayenne, and vibrant sauce make this a dish worth the effort.

Makes 6 individual puddings

1 box macaroni & cheese
1/4 c. milk
1/4 c. margarine
1 can (11 oz.) sweet corn kernels, drained
1 tbsp. minced fresh chives
1/8 tsp. cayenne pepper
Salt and pepper
1 c. milk
2 eggs, beaten lightly
3 tbsp. minced shallots
1 clove garlic, minced or pressed
1 tbsp. olive oil
1 jar (7 1/4 oz.) roasted red peppers
2 tsp. red wine vinegar

Make puddings

» Preheat oven to 350 degrees.
» Prepare macaroni & cheese with milk and margarine according to directions on the box, or use your favorite variation.
» Stir corn, chives, and cayenne into macaroni, mixing well.
» Season with salt and pepper to taste.
» Stir milk and eggs into macaroni, mixing well.
» Spray 6 ramekins or individual soufflé dishes with non-stick spray.
» Divide macaroni mixture evenly among dishes, filling them nearly to the top.
» Bake 35-45 minutes, until tops are slightly puffed, golden, and firm to the touch.
» Remove from oven and let stand 5 minutes before serving.

Make sauce

» While custards are baking, make the sauce.
» Sauté shallots and garlic in olive oil until softened.
» In a blender, puree red pepper with shallots, garlic, vinegar, and 2 tbsp. water, until smooth.
» Transfer sauce to a small saucepan, and cook over Low heat until hot.
» Season sauce with salt and pepper to taste.

Serve

» Run a thin knife around custards, and unmold onto individual serving plates.
» Spoon sauce over custards and serve.

Parmesan, Olive and Pepper Pasta Salad

Bright olive and pepper flavors liven up this pasta salad.

Serves 4

12 oz. medium pasta shells
1/3 c. olive oil
2 or 3 cloves garlic, minced or pressed
2 c. mixed greens (optional)
1 1/2 c. grated Parmesan
1/2 c. pitted, marinated olives
1/2 c. diced, roasted red peppers
1/4 c. pine nuts
Salt and pepper

» Cook the pasta in boiling water until al dente.

» While the pasta is cooking, heat the olive oil in a saucepan over Medium heat.

» Sauté garlic in oil until a few pieces begin to turn brown. Pour the oil and garlic into a cup and set aside.

» If using greens, place them in the same saucepan, and cook over Medium heat, covered, stirring occasionally, until the greens begin to wilt. Remove from heat.

» When the pasta is al dente, drain it well. Put pasta back into the pot, add the garlic olive oil, and stir well.

» Add Parmesan, olives, peppers and pine nuts to pasta, and mix well.

» Season with salt and pepper to taste.

» Salad may be served warm or cold.

Mac & Cheese Pot Stickers

1 hour

Mac & cheese pot stickers? These pot stickers are more Italian than Asian, with a tomato sauce instead of a soy sauce. Be adventurous!

Makes lots of pot stickers - decide how many you want!

1 pkg. wonton or pot sticker wrappers
1 box macaroni and cheese
1/4 c. milk
1/4 c. margarine
1/4 lb. Italian sausage
1 jar (7 1/4 oz.) roasted red peppers, diced
2 c. chicken stock
15 oz. can tomato sauce, or
1 jar tomato based pasta sauce

Make the pot stickers

» Prepare macaroni & cheese with milk and margarine according to directions on the box, or use your favorite variation.

» While macaroni is cooking, brown the sausage, breaking it into small pieces. Once browned, let it cool a little so you can handle it.

» If you're using square wonton wrappers but want the pot sticker look, you can fold them in half, corner to corner, and with scissors, round the two corners that you bring together.

» Lay out a couple of wrappers, and on the middle of each one, place a little mac & cheese, a little sausage, and a few diced red peppers. It doesn't take much!

» Wet your finger in some water and slide it around the outer quarter inch or so of the wrapper. You'll probably need to wet it twice per wrapper. Keep your work surface under the wrappers fairly dry as you go along.

» Fold the edges together, enclosing the filling. Press down to seal edges. Be careful not to overstuff, so that you keep a tight seal.

» Make as many pot stickers as you want and set them aside on wax paper.

Cook the pot stickers

» Heat tomato or pasta sauce in a small saucepan.

» Spray the bottom of a non-stick skillet with spray-on oil, or coat it evenly with a cooking oil. Preheat the pan over Medium-high heat until oil is hot but not smoking.

» Add pot stickers to pan, seam side up. They need to cook in a single layer, so you may need to cook them in batches. Push pot stickers down a little into the pan.

» Cook the pot stickers for 2-4 minutes, until you can see that the bottom of each one is frying.

» Carefully add chicken stock to skillet, until stock reaches about 1/3 of the way up the sides of the pot stickers. Don't add so much that the pot stickers float.

» Cook until the chicken stock is completely evaporated.

» Spread sauce on the serving plates, and place the pot stickers on top. Alternately, pour the sauce attractively over the pot stickers.

Mac & Cheese with Ratatouille

This colorful dish adds fresh flavors and veggies to mac & cheese. It also makes an elegant presentation without a lot of work.

Serves 3

1 box macaroni & cheese
1/4 c. milk
1/4 c. margarine
2 tbsp. olive oil
1/2 medium onion, diced
2 cloves garlic, minced or pressed
1 red bell pepper
1/2 lb. zucchini, diced
1/2 lb. yellow crookneck squash, diced
3/4 lb. tomatoes, diced
1/4 c. dry white wine
1/4 tsp. dried oregano
1/4 tsp. dried thyme
1/4 tsp. fennel seeds
Salt and pepper
1/4 c. chopped fresh basil, + 6 whole leaves
1/4 c. grated Parmesan cheese

» Prepare macaroni & cheese with milk and margarine according to directions on the box, or use your favorite variation.
» While macaroni is cooking, heat oil in a large skillet over Medium heat.
» Add onion and garlic to skillet, and cook until softened but not brown, stirring occasionally.
» Seed bell pepper. Reserve 6 thin strips for garnish, and dice the rest.
» Add the zucchini, yellow squash, and diced bell pepper to the pan. Cook, stirring occasionally, for 12 minutes.
» Add tomatoes, wine, oregano, thyme, and fennel seeds to skillet.
» Season with salt and pepper to taste.
» Cook mixture 6 minutes more, or until squash is tender.
» Remove from heat and stir in chopped basil.
» Serve macaroni & cheese topped with ratatouille.
» Sprinkle Parmesan on top, and garnish with strips of red pepper and basil leaves.

Variations

» Instead of topping the mac & cheese with ratatouille, you could just mix it all together.

Rotolino

These elegant appetizers taste as good as they look!

1 hour
× 1 hour chill

Serves 4 to 6

1 c. shredded Fontina cheese
1/2 c. finely crumbled blue cheese of your choice
4 lasagna noodles
1/2 c. chopped roasted red bell peppers
1/3 c. shelled pistachios
Extra virgin olive oil
Black pepper (optional)

» Preheat oven to 350 degrees.

» Cook the lasagna noodles in salted water, using a slow boil to minimize damage to the noodles.

» When the lasagna is al dente, drain it well, and then dry using a paper towel. Be careful not to damage the pasta.

» Return noodles to the empty pot, and gently toss with a tablespoon of olive oil to coat them.

» Spray a non-stick cookie sheet with non-stick spray.

» Find the best two undamaged noodles and lay them flat on the sheet.

» Spread the cheese over the noodles, as shown in the picture, keeping it away from the edge.

» Place the red peppers and pistachios on top of the cheese in an alternating pattern, as shown.

» Bake for 4-5 minutes, until the cheese has mostly melted. Do not let cheese melt so much that it runs out.

» Remove from oven, and let cool until you can handle it comfortably.

Madame Camembert's School of Dance

Please focus, class. The noodles and the cheese must be in perfect harmony.

» When cool enough to handle, place one of the noodles directly on top of the other, aligning the edges as best you can.

» Begin at one end and roll up the pasta. It will be a little sloppy, but go slowly and it will come out all right.

» Transfer the rolled up pasta to a plate, cover with plastic wrap, and refrigerate for at least an hour.

» Place chilled pasta on a cutting board, and using a sharp, serrated knife, carefully cut slices about 1/2-inch wide, gently sawing through pistachios you encounter.

» Place the slices on a serving plate and drizzle with a little olive oil. Serve with freshly ground pepper if desired.

Salad with Roquefort, Pears and Pecans

This is a lovely salad that pairs fresh, juicy pears with rich blue cheese.

Serves 4

1 1/2 c. dried rotini
2 tbsp. milk
2 oz. Roquefort cheese, crumbled
2 tbsp. ranch salad dressing
1/4 c. diced celery
2 tbsp. chopped pecans
1/4 c. golden raisins
2 ripe pears
8 leaves of red lettuce

» Cook the rotini in boiling, salted water until al dente. Drain and return to empty pot.
» Add milk, Roquefort, and ranch dressing to pot.
» Cook over Low heat, stirring frequently, until cheese is melted.
» Remove pasta from heat. Stir in celery, pecans, and raisins.
» Season pasta with salt and pepper to taste.
» Refrigerate pasta 15 minutes, while making the rest of the recipe.
» Quarter pears lengthwise. Remove cores, and cut into thin slices.
» On each of 4 individual serving plates, arrange 2 leaves of lettuce.
» Arrange pear slices in a fan shape on one side of each plate, and scoop pasta onto other side of the plate.

Variations

Dried cranberries work well in place of raisins.

Squash Filled with Mac & Cheese

Here's a fall and winter dish that puts the mac & cheese in the vegetables instead of the other way around.

× 1 hour 15 minutes

Serves 4 as a side dish

2 acorn squash or multi-colored squash
4 tsp. butter or margarine
Nutmeg
Salt and pepper
1 box macaroni & cheese
1/4 c. milk
1/4 c. margarine
1/4 c. + 2 tbsp. golden raisins
1/2 c. Cheddar cheese, shredded
2 tbsp. chopped walnuts

» Preheat oven to 400 degrees.

» Cut squash in half crosswise, and remove seeds.

» Line a shallow baking pan with foil.

» Set squash into dish, skin side down. Cut a slice off bottom and top of squash, as needed so they sit in baking dish without wobbling.

» Put 1 tsp. butter or margarine into each squash.

» Sprinkle each squash half with a pinch of grated nutmeg, and salt and pepper to taste.

» Bake 30 minutes.

» While squash is cooking, prepare macaroni & cheese with milk and margarine according to directions on the box, or use your favorite variation.

» Mix raisins into mac & cheese, and season with salt and pepper to taste.

» When squash has cooked 30 minutes, scoop macaroni & cheese into hollows in center of each squash.

» Spread Cheddar over each squash half, and then sprinkle walnuts on top.

» Return to oven. Bake another 20-30 minutes, or until squash is tender when pierced with a fork.

Stuffed Baked Potatoes

Serve these as a side dish with dinner, as lunch on their own, or for a snack during the football game.

1 hour

» Preheat oven to 400 degrees.

» Scrub potatoes, and prick all over with a fork.

» Bake potatoes 45 minutes, or until soft.

» While potatoes are baking, prepare macaroni & cheese with milk and margarine according to directions on the box, or use your favorite variation.

» In a large skillet, cook bacon until it's crisp.

» Drain bacon on paper towels, then crumble.

» Slice baked potatoes in half lengthwise. Scoop out the center, leaving about 1/2 inch of potato all the way around.

» Season inside of potatoes well with salt and pepper.

» Scoop macaroni & cheese into potatoes, heaping it up.

» Spread Cheddar over each potato half, and sprinkle with bacon.

» Return to oven. Bake another 10 minutes, or until cheese is thoroughly melted.

Serves 4

2 baking potatoes
1 box macaroni & cheese
1/4 c. milk
1/4 c. margarine
Salt and pepper
1 c. shredded Cheddar cheese
4 strips bacon

Variations

» Microwave version. Follow directions above, but instead of baking, microwave potatoes until they're cooked. After they're stuffed, microwave until cheese fully melts and integrates with potato.

Mac & Cheese and Music

"On the soul-food side, I can make anything: corn bread, collard greens, yams, macaroni & cheese."
- R & B great Isaac Hayes.

"I have four boxes of Kraft Dinner macaroni and cheese in my house now. I really live a glamorous lifestyle."   - Chris Robinson, The Black Crowes.

Singer Patti LaBelle can cook. Elton John is reported to love her macaroni & cheese, and she accuses him of keeping her Tupperware in the 60's.

When the Canadian band Barenaked Ladies sing "If I Had a $1,000,000", fans regularly pelt them with macaroni & cheese. The song is about a get-rich fantasy life, where boxed mac & cheese is still on the menu. Bass player Jim Creeggan complained "I get too much cheese inside my bass. It's not very easy to clear that out of it."

MAC & CHEESE AND DOGS

Mac & Cheese Stuffed Mushrooms

This recipe makes more filling than you can fit in the mushroom caps, but it's so good you'll want to eat the rest with a spoon.

Makes 16 stuffed mushrooms

1 c. macaroni & cheese (already prepared)
16 medium-sized mushrooms
1 1/2 tbsp. olive oil
1 large garlic clove, minced or pressed
2 tbsp. finely chopped onion
2 tbsp. minced fresh parsley
1/4 c. grated Parmesan cheese

» Preheat oven to 400 degrees.
» Remove mushroom stems carefully. Reserve caps, and chop stems finely.
» In a skillet, sauté garlic and onion in olive oil over Medium heat for 1 minute.
» Add chopped mushroom stems to skillet. Sauté until stems have given off their liquid and it's almost all evaporated.
» Add macaroni & cheese and parsley to skillet, and mix well.
» Place a mound of macaroni & cheese filling in each mushroom cap.
» Sprinkle mushrooms with Parmesan cheese.
» Spray a baking sheet with non-stick spray, and place mushroom caps carefully on baking sheet.
» Bake 12 to 15 minutes, or until heated through

Variations

» Add 2 strips bacon to filling, cooked until crisp and then crumbled.

Stuffed Pasilla Peppers

This dish only needs 1 cup of mac & cheese, so you can save the rest for another purpose.

Serves 4

1 box macaroni & cheese

1/4 c. milk

1/4 c. margarine

4-8 pasilla peppers, depending on size

1 c. canned or frozen corn kernels

1/2 c. canned black beans

1 c. shredded Jack cheese

Salt and pepper

1 c. salsa

Prepare components

»   The first two major steps, making the mac & cheese, and grilling the peppers, can be done at the same time.

»   Prepare macaroni & cheese with milk and margarine according to directions on the box, or use your favorite variation.

»   Turn on broiler. Put peppers on a large piece of aluminum foil, and place under broiler, about 6 inches from heat. Watch them closely to prevent burning.

»   Using a kitchen timer, check the peppers every 4 minutes, and turn over each time. Keep cooking and turning until skin is brown or a little black all over, about 12-16 minutes.

»   After the peppers are cooked on all sides, cut off the tops, and use a spoon to scrape most of the seeds out.

»   While the peppers are cooking, heat the corn and black beans together in a small saucepan.

»   When corn and beans are heated through, pour off any liquid and add the cheese, stirring until the cheese is fully melted and evenly incorporated

»   Add the macaroni & cheese, and mix well.

»   Season stuffing with salt and pepper to taste.

»   Warm the salsa if it is chilled.

Assemble and serve

»   Spoon macaroni stuffing mixture into the peppers.

»   Place peppers on individual dinner plates and spoon the salsa around the peppers.

Tuna Macaroni Salad

Here's an easy salad that's light, refreshing, attractive, and tasty. It makes a great summertime lunch, or a nice salad any time of year.

 Serves 8

1 box macaroni & cheese
1/4 c. milk
1/4 c. margarine
1 can (6 oz.) tuna packed in water, drained and flaked
1/2 c. diced celery
1/2 tsp. dried dill weed
2 scallions
1 can (2 1/4 oz.) sliced black olives
1 medium tomato

"This was a big hit with the kids – Robin had three helpings, which is virtually unheard of, and then polished off the leftovers the next day!"

- Debbie K., Prince George, British Columbia

» Make the macaroni & cheese with milk and margarine according to box directions, or your favorite variation.
» After mac & cheese is ready, stir in tuna, celery, and dill.
» Thinly slice scallions. Add white & light green portions to macaroni mixture, reserving the dark green.
» Add 1/4 cup black olives to macaroni mixture, and stir thoroughly.
» Place macaroni salad in serving bowl, and smooth top.
» Sprinkle dark green portion of scallion on top of salad.
» Cut tomato into 8 wedges, and arrange on top of salad. Garnish with additional olive slices.
» Refrigerate until serving.

Variations

Try adding one or more of the following:
» diced red or green bell pepper
» sliced sun dried tomatoes
» cucumber, seeded and diced
» cooked green beans or peas
» artichoke hearts, cut in wedges
» fresh parsley, cilantro or chives instead of the dill

Chapter (5)

BEGINNINGS
& Endings
with Mac & Cheese

Mac & Cheese Frittata

The mac & cheese lightens up the texture of the frittata, and the veggies add great flavor and color.

45 minutes

Serves 4 to 6

1 box macaroni & cheese
1/4 c. milk
1/4 c. margarine
2 tbsp. olive oil
1/4 c. finely chopped onion
1/2 c. halved and sliced zucchini
1/4 c. seeded and chopped red bell pepper
Salt and pepper
5 large eggs
1/4 c. shredded Cheddar cheese

» Prepare macaroni & cheese with milk and margarine according to directions on the box, or use your favorite variation.

» While macaroni is cooking, heat olive oil in a large skillet over Medium heat.

» Sauté onions, zucchini, and pepper until tender, about 10 minutes. During cooking, season vegetables with salt and pepper to taste.

» Beat eggs lightly in a large bowl.

» Add vegetables to bowl, along with macaroni & cheese. Stir mixture until combined well.

» In the skillet, heat remaining tbsp. oil.

» Pour egg mixture into skillet, spreading macaroni and vegetables evenly.

» Cook the frittata over Medium heat, without stirring, until set around edges but still soft in the center, about 8-10 minutes.

» Sprinkle Cheddar cheese over top of frittata.

» Broil about 4 inches from heat until cheese is melted and beginning to brown.

» Cut frittata into wedges and serve.

Macaroni & Cheese and Ham and Eggs

Here's a tasty way to fuel up on carbs for breakfast.

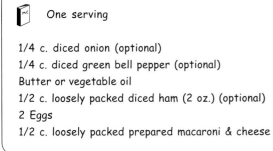

One serving

1/4 c. diced onion (optional)
1/4 c. diced green bell pepper (optional)
Butter or vegetable oil
1/2 c. loosely packed diced ham (2 oz.) (optional)
2 Eggs
1/2 c. loosely packed prepared macaroni & cheese

» Sauté the onions and peppers in oil or butter till soft.
» Add the diced ham to vegetables near the end. Keep warm in the pan.
» Lightly beat as many eggs are you are using.
» Preheat a non-stick skillet with a little butter or margarine, and cook the eggs over Medium-high heat, stirring occasionally.
» When eggs are nearly firm, add the macaroni & cheese, ham and vegetables.
» Continue cooking and stirring until eggs are done, and all ingredients are heated through.
» Season with salt and pepper to taste.

» **Note on serving size:** A standard 7 ounce box of macaroni & cheese makes about 4 cups cooked. A suitable proportion for this recipe is to use 1/2 cup of cooked macaroni & cheese per two eggs. A standard box, therefore, makes enough to go well with 16 eggs.

» **Side Note:** This is a perfect recipe for using leftover macaroni & cheese.

Variations

» Try adding some shredded Cheddar cheese in the last minute of cooking.

History of Macaroni & Cheese

Many people believe Marco Polo introduced pasta to Italy from a trip to China. In fact, dried pasta was documented in Italy in 1279, before Marco Polo returned from China in 1295.

The word macaroni is from the Italian maccheroni, and dates in English to the 16th century. Italians do bake macaroni and other pastas with cheese, but they don't make a dish with Cheddar like typical American macaroni & cheese.

A popular theory is that Thomas Jefferson introduced macaroni & cheese to the United States. He was interested in pasta, and sent away to Naples for a macaroni machine. James Hemmings, his slave chef, accompanied Jefferson to France, and made macaroni & cheese after their return.

A different story is that many English aristocrats in the 18th century visited Italy on the grand tour, and returned enamored of Italian food and fashion. The English began cooking macaroni baked with cheese and cream, and then transported this custom to the Americans.

Young English gentlemen who followed the outlandish French and Italian fashions wore pouffy wigs, tiny hats, ruffles and tight pants, and formed London's Macaroni Club. In the well-known song, Yankee Doodle "stuck a feather in his hat and called it Macaroni". This was poking fun at Americans who followed the same fashion.

In the US, macaroni and cheese became popular as a cheap, tasty and filling meal. By the 1920's, it was common in diners. In New York's Horn & Hardart Automats, a nickel would get you a plate of macaroni & cheese from behind one of the little glass panels.

In 1937, Kraft came out with their boxed Macaroni and Cheese Dinner, ushering in a new generation of this favorite dish.

YANKEE DOODLE

Mac & Cheese Jam Tarts

These tarts look good and taste great. They're rich enough that one tart will make a good breakfast for most people. Try them when you've got an active day planned.

 Serves 6

2 c. dried small pasta shells
2 tbsp. butter
2 c. shredded cheese (Havarti or Gouda)
1/2 c. milk
1 egg
Raspberry or apricot jam
6 4-inch tart pans

» Preheat oven to 350 degrees.
» Cook the pasta shells 8 minutes, or according to package directions.
» When pasta is done, drain and return to pan.
» Add butter and cheese to pasta, and mix thoroughly.
» Fill tart pans with pasta mixture, patting it down evenly.
» Whisk together milk and egg until combined well.
» Pour milk mixture over pasta in tart pans, dividing it evenly between the tarts.
» Place tart pans on a cookie sheet. Bake for 25-30 minutes, or until they begin to turn a pale gold on top.
» Remove tarts from oven and cool 1 hour on a rack.
» Cover tarts with plastic wrap, place in refrigerator and chill overnight.
» In the morning, remove tarts from pans. Spread jam generously on top of each tart, and serve.

Variations

» **Toppings** – Instead of jam, try putting honey, orange marmalade, or fresh fruit on top.

» **Camping** – These are excellent for camping! Make them at home, and then pack the tarts in their pans so they don't get squished. Pack the jam in a separate container. In camp, just unmold and add topping, and you've got a quick, filling breakfast. Luxury camp food!

Macaroni Apple Crisp

× 1 hour 30 minutes

Apples and Cheddar go together like ... well, like apples and Cheddar! It's a delicious combination, and the spiced topping makes this a terrific dessert for fall and winter.

Serves 6

1 box macaroni & cheese
1/4 c. milk
1/4 c. margarine
3 green apples
2 tsp. lemon juice
1/4 c. granulated sugar
1/4 c. brown sugar, packed
1/4 tsp. ground nutmeg
1/4 tsp. cinnamon
Pinch of salt
3/8 c. flour
1/2 stick butter, cut into bits
1/4 c. chopped walnuts

» Preheat oven to 350 degrees.
» Prepare macaroni & cheese with milk and margarine according to directions on the box, or use your favorite variation.
» Peel and core apples, cut into 1/4-inch slices, and chop into pieces.
» Sprinkle lemon juice over apples, and toss thoroughly to keep from turning brown.
» Mix apples with macaroni & cheese. Place mixture in a shallow 2-qt. baking pan.
» Mix sugars, spices, salt and flour in a bowl.
» Add butter to sugar mixture, and work it in with a pastry cutter or your fingers, until the mixture resembles a coarse meal.
» Stir walnuts into sugar mixture.
» Spread sugar mixture over the top of the apples and macaroni, patting it down evenly.
» Cover baking pan with foil, and bake 30 minutes.
» Remove foil, and bake 30 minutes more, until topping is light brown.
» Serve warm.

Honey Pepper Feta Bake

Ever tried black pepper with dessert? This simple and delicious recipe is really something special!

 Serves 6

8 oz. dried medium shell pasta
10 oz. Feta cheese, crumbled
1/4 c. + 2 tbsp. milk
Freshly ground black or rainbow peppercorns
4 tbsp. honey, or to taste

» Preheat oven to 350 degrees.

» Cook pasta in boiling, salted water until al dente.
  Drain, then return to empty pot.

» Add Feta cheese and milk to pot. Cook over Medium
  heat, stirring frequently.

» Season with pepper to taste. Continue cooking and stirring until cheese is melted and evenly
  distributed.

» Put shells on individual serving plates. Drizzle with honey, and sprinkle with a little more freshly
  ground pepper.

» Serve warm.

Chapter 6

Mac & Cheese
BLOOPERS
and Other Oddities

Bloopers

Mac & Cheese Burger

» *Basic boxed macaroni and cheese – frozen into a patty*

If you froze mac and cheese into a hamburger shaped patty could you then grill it and eat it like a hamburger? ... NO!

Mac and Cheese Waffles

» *Basic boxed macaroni and cheese*

Ok, this was an idea whose time just never came. After lots of smoke, trying to get the pasta to hold together, we had to concede this just makes a mess.

Baked Kiwi with Shells

» *Pasta shells, kiwi, olive oil, Parmesan*

Fresh kiwi with macaroni and cheese is surprisingly delicious (see Quick Hits-Fruit). Baked kiwi, it turns out, tastes remarkably like ... rhubarb! Yuck!

Noodle Pancake

» *Spaghetti, olive oil*

This was supposed to come out something like a hash brown, and be served with apple sauce, like the German dish, reibekuchen. Unlike the crispiness of browned potatoes, browned spaghetti is unavoidably just hard.

Fettucine Terrine

» *Fettucine, Parmesan, egg, sausage, red peppers, olives*

This wasn't a real terrine, but it was supposed to sort of look like one after it was cooked and sliced. It actually tasted pretty good. It just looked really awful.

Bird's Nest

» *Spaghetti, egg, olive oil, Parmesan*

The reasoning behind this dish has been lost.

Mac and Cheese Snack Treats

» *Basic boxed macaroni and cheese*

The idea here was to create little mac and cheese snacks that you could pack for a hike or something. Make the mac and cheese, then bake it. Hard, hard, hard!

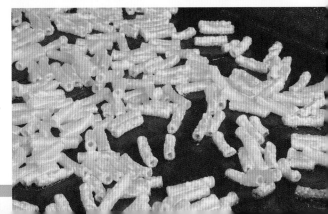

Serving Options

The mac and cheese weight loss plan. For mac and cheese lovers on a diet – save calories!

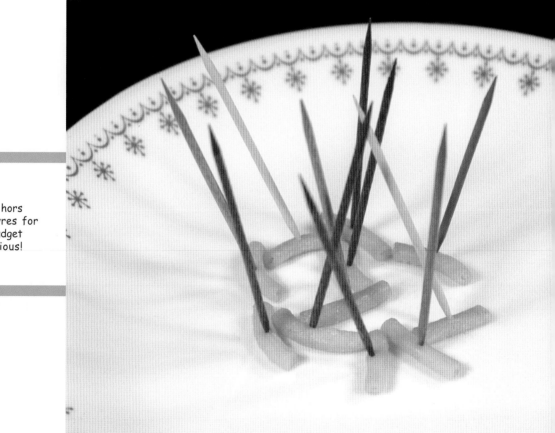

Tasty hors d'oeuvres for the budget conscious!

Who needs a fork? The cross-cultural approach to eating mac and cheese.

For a nice, cool summer treat, how about macaroni and cheese ice cream!

And last but not least, the classic serving maneuver!

Colored Mac & Cheese
for Special Occasions

For Valentine's, is the way to a man's heart through his stomach?

Try some green cheese for St. Patrick's Day.

Black mac is truly ghoulish - scary stuff for Halloween!

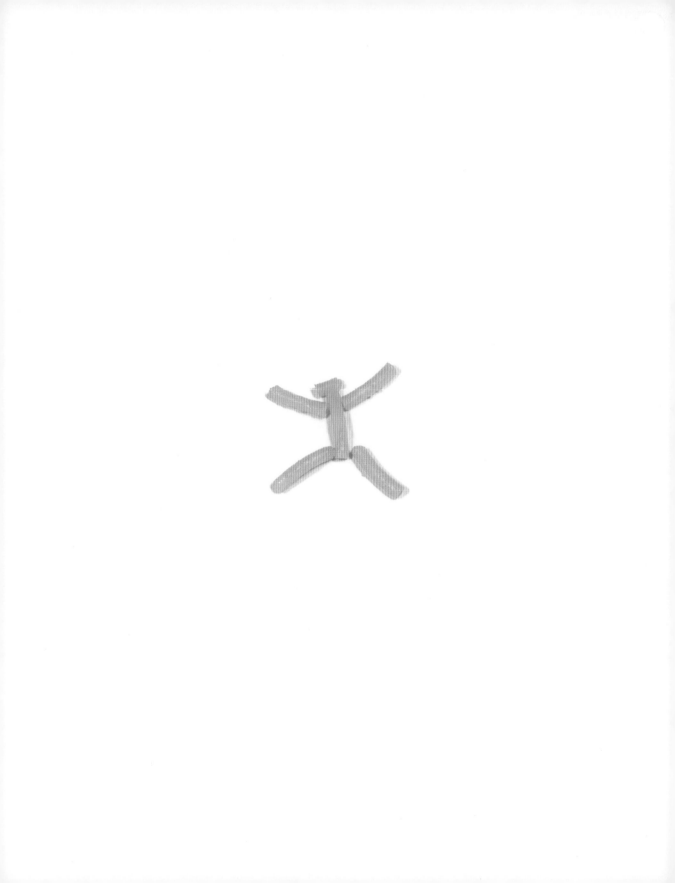

Mac & Cheese Gifts
for Family, Friends and Yourself!

Featured ITEMS

Want a cute gift for the kids? Check out this Dr. Frank t-shirt. Perfect for mac & cheese fans!

How about a Happy Food baseball cap for Dad? Food makes him happy, & so will this!

Liven up someone's lunch hour with this funny Food Pyramid lunch box!

Product Groups

| T-shirts | Other Apparel | Kitchen | Hats | Fun Stuff |

Go to
maccheese.com
to order Gifts and Goods.

Designs

Index